Freedom

from

Ego

Games

Freedom

from

Ego

Games

KIM MICHAELS

MORE TO LIFE PUBLISHING

www.morepublish.com

For foreign and translation rights,

contact info@ morepublish.com

ISBN: 978-9949-518-31-9

Series ISBN: 978-9949-518-21-0

The information and insights in this book should not be considered as a form of therapy, advice, direction, diagnosis, and/or treatment of any kind. This information is not a substitute for medical, psychological, or other professional advice, counseling and care. All matters pertaining to your individual health should be supervised by a physician or appropriate health-care practitioner. No guarantee is made by the author or the publisher that the practices described in this book will yield successful results for anyone at any time. They are presented for informational purposes only, as the practice and proof rests with the individual.

For more information: *www.askrealjesus.com*.

CONTENTS

The ego can never
experience Gnosis,
for if it did,
it would instantly
cease to exist.

INTRODUCTION

This book is part of the *From the Heart of Jesus* series, which means the content is given through a process of direct revelation by the ascended master Jesus. For more information on ow Jesus brings forth these teachings, see the first book in this series, *The Mystical Teachings of Jesus* or the websites *www.ascendedmasterlight.com* and *www.askrealjesus.com*.

This book is the second in a three-part series on the ego. It will describe the games that the ego creates in order to keep your attention focused on the ongoing human struggle and prevent you from realizing who you really are and why you are here.

The first book, *Freedom From Ego Illusions*, gives a general overview of how the ego distorts your vision and how you can begin to free yourself from its illusions. It will be helpful to have read the first book before reading this one, although it is not absolutely necessary.

The third book, *Freedom From Ego Dramas*, will describe the dramas created by the ego in order to distort your inner desire to make a positive difference on this planet. It will explain why so many people have been pulled into fighting for a cause by killing other people and why this has led to so many atrocities throughout history.

The ego was born
from separation,
and it is incapable of
seeing beyond it
or even questioning it.

1 | MAKING LIFE DECISIONS OR DEATH DECISIONS

We have now reached a turning point in my discourses on the ego. My first nine discourses form the Alpha polarity. My last discourse on magnificent confusion forms the nexus of the figure-eight, and we will now enter the lower figure, the Omega polarity. [The previous discourses are included in the book *Freedom From Ego Illusions*]

The first discourses presented the overall view, the big picture, so that you have a foundation for knowing that you are more than the ego. It was an attempt to show you the forest without focusing on the individual trees. Why did I start out this way? Because you are not only a person who is lost in the forest, you are a person who has grown up in the forest. Your upbringing has not given you a clear understanding of the real cause that makes your life an ongoing struggle.

I had to start out by showing you that you are lost but that there is something outside the forest. It is not until you recognize yourself as lost that you can start looking for a way out instead of feeling hopeless – or even content – in the shadow of the trees. You now understand that the core of your identity is the Conscious You and that you are MORE than the earthly identity built by your ego.

You should also recognize that you already know you are more than the ego because it is the Conscious You who has studied my previous discourses on the ego. You have done so only because you want to be more than what you are right now. You don't really think it was your ego that compelled you to read these long and somewhat complex discourses on the ego, do you? You should allow yourself to recognize that you already know there is something outside the ego forest.

However, having a mental image of the forest is not the same as being outside that forest. You still have to follow the trail that leads you out, and for a time your vision of what is outside will be blocked by a number of individual trees. In this book we will look at the individual trees, namely the games that the ego has constructed in order to keep you trapped in the forest. The strategy of the ego is to get you so entangled in the branches of one or more individual trees that you forget about the trail.

Let me assure you that having made it this far, especially if you have recognized that you are in a state of magnificent confusion, is an accomplishment. My first discourses were actually designed to act as a filter to filter out those who are not ready to let go of their egos. I am in no way passing judgment upon such people; I am simply stating the fact that not everyone is ready to see through the ego and let it die bit by bit.

Virtually every human being on this planet is somewhat blinded by the ego. Most people are not ready to even acknowledge the existence of the ego, let alone take a long look in the mirror and recognize: "I have an ego, and I need to rise above it!" Such people will have taken one of the "easy ways out" that I offered between the lines in the first discourses, and their egos will have found an excuse for not continuing. Anyone who starts the series will have had certain seeds planted, and in good time they will sprout and come to the surface of awareness so that the person can take another look at the ego.

If you have sincerely studied my previous discourses, you are ready to begin looking at the specific games that your own ego is playing. You have already overcome some of these games or you would still be so identified with the ego that you would not be open to this teaching. As I describe the games, I hope you will begin to recognize that as a spiritual seeker, you have risen above some of the most destructive ego games.

I hope this will give you some encouragement in realizing that you might be further along on the path than you thought. Even if you have only overcome the very lowest ego game, you are still in a much better place than those who are trapped in that game. I hope you will recognize that if you have overcome one ego game, you can overcome them all, for they are truly all cut from the same cloth. As I will explain further, the ego has only one game that comes in numerous disguises, some more subtle than others. Once you see the basic strategy of the ego, you can more easily expose the rest of its games.

I hope you will honestly look at yourself, recognize which games you have left behind and build a positive momentum. As you build this momentum, you should be able to acknowledge when you come to the first game that you have not yet – completely – overcome. Then you can use your momentum to avoid a negative reaction – such as guilt or denial – and simply acknowledge that since you have already risen above one or more games, you can surely rise above this next one as well.

As you continue to build on your accomplishments, you will reinforce the momentum until it becomes an unstoppable force that pulls you through the forest and simply cuts down the trees that are in your way. Before you know it, you will see the light filtering through the trees, and one day you will break through the last brush and enter the open field where your eyes can finally see the horizon of Being.

Think about what it is like to be lost in a forest. The biggest problem is that you have no absolute point of reference, you have no horizon but only a very limited field of view. You only see trees and have no way of knowing which direction to follow in order to get out of the forest. As you cut down the individual trees, you will eventually catch a glimpse of the horizon, and now you will have a firm direction to follow. In the beginning it might seem like overcoming the ego is hopeless, but if you keep overcoming the individual ego games, you will one day break through and catch a glimpse of your own higher being. From then on, you will never again be completely lost in the forest.

The master game of the ego

Although I will describe the individual games used by the ego, I will start out by describing the master game. You may not be able to clearly see this game at this point, but I want to plant the seed in your mind so that it can germinate and eventually break through to your conscious awareness.

As I explained in my first discourses, the Conscious You created the ego by deciding that it would no longer make decisions. This is illustrated in the old fairy tale about the sleeping beauty. The princess is the Conscious You and one day she falls victim to a plot hatched by the evil Godmother, namely the prince of this world. The princess falls asleep and an impenetrable forest grows up around her castle. The forest, of course, is the ego and the individual trees are the illusions of the ego, the ego games. One day a prince comes by, penetrates the forest and kisses the princess, who awakens. The prince symbolizes the Living Christ who can take on many forms, both as an outer teacher and as the inner teacher of your Christ self. Regardless of the form, the Living Christ always serves to awaken the Conscious You to the need to come up higher.

In the fairy tale, the prince and the princess live happily ever after, and here is where the fairy tale departs from reality. In the real world, the Conscious You is not home free by being awakened. It – you – must personally cut down all of the trees that surround the castle, and only then will you live happily ever after.

The master strategy of the ego involves two elements. The first one is that the ego will do anything it can to prevent the Conscious You from awakening to the realization that there must be more to your identity. For the majority of human beings, this strategy is still working, and they still identify themselves completely with the identity that the ego has built in the material world. The fact that you are reading this means that you are a spiritual seeker, and thus your ego's first strategy has failed. You know there is more to your identity and you are actively looking for it.

You are now the target for the ego's second strategy, which is to prevent you from clearing the thorny trees around the castle. Each tree represents a decision, a decision based on the mind of anti-christ, the mind of duality and separation. This is where I would like to leave the fairy-tale analogy behind and instead refer to the image of a spiral staircase. Each decision that was based on the mind of anti-christ took you further down the spiral staircase, the staircase that leads into the darkness of separation from your higher being. This is what the Bible refers to as "the valley of the shadow of death" (Proverbs 23:4).

The separation from your I AM Presence and your true sense of identity truly is the consciousness of spiritual death. The decisions based on the illusions of the mind of anti-christ brought you further into the consciousness of death. We might say that each of these decisions was a Death decision. One kiss from the prince is not enough to raise you out of the shadow of death. You must consciously walk the staircase and undo each of the decisions that brought you down the staircase. This is precisely what the ego will do everything in its power to prevent you from doing.

In order to take a step up the spiral staircase, you must come to see through the dualistic illusion that brought you down to that step. You can do this only by seeing the Christ truth that counteracts the illusion, the truth that makes you free. You must then choose the truth of Christ over the "truth" of anti-christ. You must choose life over death. I would like to call each of these decisions a "LIFE decision."

The ego will do anything to prevent you from making these LIFE decisions. In order to accomplish this overall goal, the ego – and the forces of anti-christ – have invented a number of subtle games. The goal is to keep you entangled with a particular illusion so that you cannot let go of it and rise to the next step on the path.

What is a LIFE decision?

When I talk about LIFE decisions, I am not talking about minor decisions, such as whether to bring an umbrella or what to have for lunch. Nor am I talking about big decisions in your material life, such as what career to pursue or what person to marry. I am talking about the kind of decisions that affect how you see yourself, God, the world and the relationship between these three factors in your life. I am talking about decisions that affect your sense of identity.

As I explained in the previous discourses, when you descend one step on the spiral staircase, your old identity dies

and a new one is born. In order to ascend one step, the old –
human – identity must die and a new more spiritual one must
be born. That is why I said:

> 5 Jesus answered, Verily, verily, I say unto thee, Except a
> man be born of water and of the Spirit, he cannot enter
> into the kingdom of God.
> 6 That which is born of the flesh is flesh; and that which
> is born of the Spirit is spirit. (John, Chapter 3)

This spiritual rebirth requires you to voluntarily and consciously – if it is not conscious, it cannot be voluntary – let the
old human identity die and accept that you are reborn into a
higher spiritual sense of identity. To make this less abstract, let
me give an example.

Many people struggle with alcoholism and use various programs, such as Alcoholics Anonymous, to combat this condition. Some manage to stop drinking by using the force of
conscious will to suppress the urge to drink. This is commend-
able, but it comes at a price, namely that you must struggle to
uphold the decision, often for the rest of your life. An organization such as AA maintains that you are an alcoholic for life
and that you must continue to suppress the urge to drink. I am
not denouncing this approach for people at a certain level, but
there is a higher approach. [For more about AA and addic-
tions, see www.*ascendedmasteranswers.com*.]

There is only one reason why you could become susceptible to alcoholism in the first place, namely that you have
accepted a sense of identity as a human being who has no
real purpose to life and who is powerless to overcome certain
problems. If you can't overcome a problem (to stop the pain)
and if you really are not worth anything, it is okay to dull the
pain through alcohol.

You then gradually slide into a physical and emotional addiction, but one day the Conscious You wakes up and realizes this cannot go on or you will die. You go into a treatment program and use the force of will to suppress what is seen as the cause of the problem, namely the urge to drink. However, the real cause is your sense of identity as a basically worthless human being whose life has no higher purpose and who can never overcome past mistakes.

The real solution is to transcend that state of consciousness, which you can do by internalizing the Christ truth that you are a unique, spiritual being who is infinitely loved by God and who came to earth for a specific spiritual purpose. Once you accept this new sense of identity – once you let the old identity die and are spiritually reborn – you will see that you are worthy and that your life has a mission that is far too important to let alcohol stand in the way of its fulfillment.

You have not simply suppressed the urge to drink – which is only the effect and not the cause – but you have accepted a higher sense of identity. For the new person that you now are, drinking is simply unthinkable. It is not even an option, and the ego and the prince of this world have no way to tempt you into drinking. You are so focused on your mission that you do not even notice their temptations. (This leads them to stop and attempt to come up with another kind of temptation that works at your new level of consciousness. Nevertheless, you have still made significant progress and it has become harder for them to tempt you.)

Do you now see the overall strategy of the ego? You have descended the staircase by accepting a lower sense of identity than your true identity, which is that you are a unique spiritual being. You have accepted that you are a human being with certain limitations. The ego is trying to prevent you from letting go of a limited sense of identity and accepting a higher one. It does this by either keeping you in spiritual blindness (so you don't see your limitations or the alternative) or making you so attached to your current sense of identity that you are not willing to let go of it.

Your current sense of identity is based on something in this world, it is a worldly or material sense of identity. The ego is trying to keep you so entangled with or attached to the "things of this world" that you either cannot see or cannot accept your true spiritual identity. The ego seeks to accomplish this through the individual ego games, each of which is designed to keep you so focused on something in the material world that you cannot or will not look beyond it. You are not willing to give up your limited sense of identity in order to rise to a broader sense of identity. You are not able or willing to let go of your belief that you are the lower identity and that there is nothing more to you than what that identity specifies.

How did you descend the staircase of life?

Let us now consider how you descended the staircase that led you to your present level of consciousness. Here is where the fairy tale – and even the Bible – gives an incorrect description of the process. The Bible describes the Fall of Man as one momentous event. In a sense it is true that losing contact with your spiritual teacher was a momentous event, but it happened as the result of a gradual process.

Many religions and many New Age teachings present the Fall of Man as one event and they present the solution – salvation or whatever it is called – the same way. This is one of the illusions created by the prince of this world. He wants you to believe that if only you belong to the right Christian church and believe all its doctrines, I – or rather the church's idolatrous image of Christ – will one day appear in the sky and save you. Or he wants you to believe that if only you are loving and kind to everyone, you will one day spontaneously wake up and be enlightened.

Both philosophies – and the many others that spring from the same consciousness – have the same goal, namely to pacify you so that you do not realize the true key to salvation, spiritual growth, enlightenment or whatever you want to call it. That key is to understand the mechanics of how you descend and ascend the spiral staircase and the role of LIFE decisions.

The consciousness of anti-christ is subtle, which means that the Fall did not happen as the result of one decision on your part. You gradually started experimenting with the dualistic mind, and you gradually descended the spiral staircase. At some point the Conscious You did make the momentous decision that it would no longer be in command of your life, but most people did this without fully realizing what was at stake. They had already become so partially blinded by the duality of the mind of anti-christ that they did not fully understand what had happened. They did not understand that they had just made the quintessential Death decision.

Compare this to descending a staircase. If you walk down the steps, each step will send a jolt up your legs, and you know you have descended one step. You experience each step as a discrete and distinct event and you know you have gone one step down. Now imagine that you lie down on the staircase and allow gravity to pull your body down. You simply slide down the steps and because your body spans several steps, it becomes harder to realize that you have descended a step and that this is a discrete event. After all, which step did you just descend, the one under your head or the one under your feet? When you do not clearly see that you have taken a step down, you can slide quite far down the spiral staircase before you even realize what has happened.

When you descended the staircase of consciousness, you did not clearly see what was happening. You did not realize that each step was a discrete event that caused your old sense of identity to die and a new – more limited one – to be born. The reason why you did not see this was that you were blinded by the dualistic logic of the mind of anti-christ, as Eve was blinded by the serpent in the Garden of Eden when he said: "Thou shalt not surely die!"

This is the very same lie that is behind each of the steps you have taken down the staircase. You think that you will not surely die by making a death decision. After all, you have already gone part of the way suggested by the ego and you are still alive so why not follow the ego a bit further? This is the logic that allowed you to slide down the spiral staircase until you could no longer see the exit door at the top and even forgot there is something at the top of the staircase. This is when the Conscious You accepted a sense of identity as a human being instead of a spiritual being.

Here is where we must once again correct the fairy tale. It is true that the Conscious You is asleep, but only metaphorically speaking. You are asleep in the sense that you do not see the reality of life, namely that you are more than a material, human being and that the world is more than the material universe. You are not asleep in the sense that you are unconscious. You are painfully aware of the consequences of the ego-based decisions and you cannot escape experiencing those consequences. Here is where we need to take a closer look at what exactly it means that the Conscious You stopped making decisions.

Making decisions without making decisions

In my previous discourses, I said that at some point the Conscious You decided that it would no longer make decisions, and it allowed the ego to make decisions for you. This is true, but there is a deeper understanding that we now need to uncover.

The fact is that there are some decisions that can be made by the ego and there are some decisions that can only be made by the Conscious You. The Conscious You is an extension of your I AM Presence and a spark of God's Being. It is sent into the material world with the command to multiply and have dominion. This means that you must multiply your sense of identity as a co-creator, and only the Conscious You can make decisions about your sense of identity. Only the Conscious You can make a Death decision – a decision that leads you to a lower sense of identity – or a LIFE decision—a decision that leads you to a higher sense of identity. The ego cannot make such decisions, but it can influence how the Conscious You makes such decisions.

To illustrate this, consider a company that is owned by one person. The owner does not want to make all the day-to-day decisions and has hired a CEO to run the business while he spends time in his private office or in his country club. The CEO can make most of the decisions related to running the business, but some decisions must still be made by the owner. One year the CEO makes some bad decisions and the company loses money, yet he does not admit this to the owner. Instead, he comes up with a plan that makes it seem like it was market conditions that led to the loss, and if only the owner will approve a loan from the bank, the company will regroup and be much stronger next year.

Because the owner really does not want to run the company himself, he believes the CEO and approves the loan. This obviously takes the company one step down the ladder of debt, but the owner thinks it will only be a temporary setback and he again retreats into his private world. The next year the company is still not showing a profit, but again the CEO comes up with a convincing plan and the owner – who really doesn't want to leave his private world – approves another loan.

Obviously, this process can continue for as long as the owner believes the CEO. As long as the CEO can avoid something that shakes the owner's trust, he can get away with quite a lot, and the company can slide into hopeless debt before the owner realizes what is going on. Once the situation gets so bad that the owner can no longer ignore it, he will have to wake up and run the company himself. However, what will it take to get to that point? That depends on the balance between the owner's desire to stay in his private world and his desire to avoid having the company go down. As long as there is no distinct event that shatters the owner's illusion, the slide can continue indefinitely.

What is the real problem here? Although the owner has retreated from running the company, he is not completely isolated. He still feels the consequences of the company not making a profit and he still has to make the most important decisions. Although he might feel as if he is no longer making decisions, this is only an illusion. He is still making the Death decisions that take the company to a distinctly lower level, yet what he is not doing is taking charge of gathering the information upon which these decisions are based. He allows the CEO to present to him a selective picture of the situation, and then he bases his decisions on the image presented by the CEO.

This is the exact dynamic between the Conscious You and the ego. The Conscious You decides that it no longer wants to be in command of your life so it allows the ego to make the day-to-day decisions. The ego cannot decide on your sense of identity so the ego can only make decisions within the framework of how the Conscious You sees itself. The ego's decisions are based on the duality consciousness, which means they will inevitably lead to undesirable consequences.

The Conscious You will experience these consequences, but the ego will present you with a "company report" that makes it seem like this is just a temporary setback. You are the victim of circumstances beyond your control, but if only you will make the decision recommended by the ego, you will see that things will get better. The ego will present you with a view of the situation that is based on dualistic thinking. The ego really believes its solution will work, but in reality a solution based on the duality consciousness cannot solve problems created by the duality consciousness.

If you still do not want to take back the responsibility for running the company, you might believe the ego. You will then make a Death decision that takes you down to a distinctly lower sense of identity. You might not realize what is happening, but the ego will now begin to make decisions based on this lower sense of identity. By accepting a lower sense of identity, you have given the ego more freedom to act, and this will lead to even more unpleasant consequences. You have already set the stage for the next crisis.

The mechanics are simple. You make a Death decision that takes you to a lower level of identity. The ego now takes over and makes the minor decisions based on this new sense of identity. Each of these decisions leads to unpleasant consequences, and in order to escape those consequences, you will – as long as you refuse to take command of your life – make another Death decision that takes you further down the staircase.

When it comes time for the next company report, the ego will present a rosy picture that makes it seem like it is not the ego's fault, and certainly not *your* fault. Sure, things are tough right now, but they are sure to get better. In the meantime, why don't you – the new human being – simply make yourself comfortable by taking advantage of the pleasures the material world has to offer. Stop worrying about the purpose of life and simply have a little fun. Live a little—until you have to die some more.

Take note of a subtle mechanism. By accepting the identity as a human being, the Conscious You actually gets a sense of reprieve because this identity implies that you are a powerless being who is the victim of circumstances – the material world – beyond your control. It is inevitable that bad things happen, and this only reinforces the Conscious You's decision not to take charge—for how can you take command when you are just a powerless human being?

The only way out

Once you have forgotten your higher identity, you cannot see any way out of your dilemma. You do not understand that the unpleasant consequences are the inevitable result of decisions based on the duality consciousness. You have forgotten that there is an alternative to this state of consciousness so you think the only way to escape the unpleasant consequences is to make better dualistic decisions.

You think you can solve your problems without transcending your current sense of identity—which is the source of your problems. This is precisely what your ego and the prince of this world want you to keep believing. They want you to believe in the illusion that you can solve a problem with the same state of consciousness that created the problem (which is what *they* believe).

At some point, the Conscious You will experience such severe consequences that it will wake up and say: "I can't keep doing this anymore; I have to change something." Even after this awakening, the ego will do anything to prevent you from realizing the reality I have just described. That reality has the following components:

• Only the Conscious You can make LIFE and Death decisions, decisions that take you up or down the staircase of identity.

• You have descended that staircase because you made Death decisions.

• You made those decisions because you allowed the ego to gather the information upon which you based the decisions.

• Because the ego can see only the mind of anti-christ, all of its information was dualistic in nature and could only create more problems.

• The only way out is to start making LIFE decisions.

• Such decisions must be based on the reality of the Christ mind rather than on the illusions of the mind of anti-christ.

• Only the Conscious You can access the Christ mind. The ego can never do so.

• The Conscious You always has the option to reach for the mind of Christ. No matter how far you have descended on the staircase, you can still ask for guidance and you will receive it. When the student is ready, the teacher will always appear, and the teacher will give the student exactly what is needed to take the very next step up the spiral staircase. The challenge for you is to recognize the teacher and be willing to follow directions.

The problem is that before you can make use of this "open door that no man can shut," you – meaning the Conscious You – must decide to take back responsibility for your life. You must take back responsibility for making LIFE decisions and you must take back responsibility for gathering the information upon which you base those decisions. You must refuse to allow the ego to back you into a corner where it seems like you have to make decisions based on two extremes that are both defined by the mind of anti-christ. You must refuse to be manipulated into a situation where it seems like your only option is to choose the lesser evil. You must take back your responsibility to discern between the truth of Christ and the illusions of anti-christ.

Once you have made the decision not to take command, you allow the ego to provide the information upon which you make the big decisions, and you slide down the staircase without realizing what is happening. You experience it as a blur rather than as a string of discrete events, each one causing the death of the old you and the birth of a new you. However, you cannot ascend the staircase the same way. You cannot simply slide up the staircase—you must walk by your own efforts. You cannot expect a spiritual teacher to pull you up the staircase as the ego pulled you down. You must stand up and decide to walk by your own effort.

The real key is to realize that walking up the staircase requires you to take a number of discrete and distinct steps. In order to climb to the next step, you must remove both feet from the previous step, meaning that you must decide to leave that step behind forever. This requires you to willingly let the old sense of identity die and allow yourself to be reborn into a new sense of identity. This is what Paul described:

22 That ye put off concerning the former conversation
the old man, which is corrupt according to the deceitful
lusts;
23 And be renewed in the spirit of your mind;
24 And that ye put on the new man, which after God is
created in righteousness and true holiness. (Ephesians,
Chapter 4)

For each step you take up the spiral staircase, you must
make a decision. This decision must be based on the following:

•   You see that what brought you to your current step
on the staircase was a decision that *you* made.

•   You see that the decision was based on the illusions
of the mind of anti-christ presented by the ego.

•   You see why this illusion is out of touch with reality
and why it could only lead to unpleasant consequences.

•   You see this because you have recognized the truth
of Christ that makes you free from the illusion.

•   You now consciously and with no regrets or attach-
ments choose to let go of the illusion and accept and
internalize the truth of Christ.

By making this LIFE decision, you have allowed the old
"you" to die and you have been spiritually reborn into a new
sense of identity. This does not mean you are now saved and
will live happily ever after. It means you have ascended one
step on the spiral staircase, and you are now ready to face the
next challenge. Only when you have faced every decision that

brought you down the staircase, will you reach the top and live happily ever after.

The ultimate LIFE decision

Let me summarize what I have revealed in this discourse: You can sleepwalk your way down the spiral staircase of life, but you cannot sleepwalk your way back up! You can get down by making unconscious decisions, but you can get back up only by making conscious decisions.

Let me return to the analogy of the owner of a company. After several years of bad financial results, the owner finally wakes up and realizes his CEO has fed him a distorted view of the company's situation. He now faces the crucial decision of whether to take back charge of the company or whether to simply fire the bad CEO and hire another one so he can continue to retreat into his private world. He decides to do the latter and hires a new CEO. He is unaware that it is actually the old CEO who has taken on a disguise and has presented himself as a different person.

As a spiritual seeker, you have already made some LIFE decisions, and for each decision, you fired the ego which caused you to rise to a higher sense of identity. The problem is that the ego will immediately change its disguise and present itself as a capable CEO who can run your new company for you. Many spiritual seekers have made significant progress, yet they have not yet come to the point of making the ultimate LIFE decision.

This decision is the firm commitment that you will take charge of your life and that you will remain in charge. You will make the important decisions and you will take responsibility for attaining the vision of Christ before you make such decisions. You will keep making one LIFE decision after another, and you will keep doing so until you reach the top of the spiral staircase. You will never again allow your ego to talk you into abandoning your responsibility to discern between the reality of Christ and the unreality of anti-christ.

Now, before you become discouraged and start feeling like it is an insurmountable task to overcome all of the ego's illusions, let me make it clear what you are up against. You might take an honest look at yourself and see that you still have a ways to go before you are free of the ego. In your current state of confusion it might seem very difficult to see through the ego's illusions. Who ever said you have to see through the ego's illusions all at once or that you have to do so with your current level of consciousness?

Why do you think I keep talking about a spiral staircase? The key to climbing a staircase is to take one step at a time, and all you need to do is focus on two steps at a time—the step you are on right now and the one right above it. You don't need to look at the top step, and you certainly don't need to climb the staircase by taking one giant leap. You simply keep putting one foot above the other, and as long as you keep taking one doable step at a time, you will make it to the top. The ego can stop you only by preventing you from rising above a certain step.

Let us say that the spiral staircase has 33 steps. You take stock of your life and realize you are on Step 10. At this stage you do not have the Christ discernment and insight to see through the ego illusion that prevents you from rising from Step 32 to Step 33. Yet you don't have to see through that illusion right now. You only have to see through the illusion that prevents you from rising from Step 10 to Step 11. I can assure you that you do have what it takes to dismiss that illusion. You simply need to ask for Christ vision, and if you ask with an open mind, you will receive an answer.

It is a spiritual law that when the student is ready, the teacher will appear. The teacher may appear as the inner teacher of your Christ self or as an outer teacher that might have a variety of disguises. The teacher will always find a way to present you with the insight you need in order to rise to the next step. If your mind is open, you will recognize the Divine direction and use it to rise to a higher level of identity. Once you have that higher sense of identity, you will have what it takes to dismiss the next ego-illusion and take another step.

What is the ego's master strategy? It is to prevent you from making the *ultimate* LIFE decision, but also to prevent you from making the *next* LIFE decision. It is precisely in order to accomplish this goal that the ego and the prince of this world have come up with a number of games that are designed to keep you stuck at a particular step. As you begin to study these games, you will see that you have already overcome some of them. This should give you the inner knowing that you can overcome all of them by simply taking one step at a time.

I realize that it can still seem like climbing the staircase is an overwhelming task. The fact that you are reading this teaching proves that you are not at the lowest step—the level of a cave man or psychotic criminal. How did you rise to your current step? You did so because the Living Christ in some form reached out to you and you heeded the call. You accepted the teacher's directions and used them to make a LIFE decision that brought you one step higher. You continued to do this until you reached your current step.

So far, the teacher has been there for you every step of the way—and you have followed the teacher's instructions. Based on this fact, is it rational to doubt that the teacher will be there for each of the following steps as well? Is it rational to doubt that you can and will follow the teacher as you have already done? Why not simply realize that you have already stepped on to the true path, and as long as you keep following it by reaching for the higher vision of Christ, you will make it all the way home. You can therefore accept the message in the full quote that I gave in part earlier:

> Yea, though I walk through the valley of the shadow of death, I will fear no evil: for thou art with me; thy rod and thy staff they comfort me. (Proverbs 23:4)

Trust that the teacher will be with you each step of the way, and as long as you keep moving, you will make it to the goal. As the old saying goes: "A journey of a thousand miles begins with one step." However, the journey is completed only by those who keep taking the next step.

❧

2 | HOW TO MAKE LIFE DECISIONS

I understand that many people will read my latest discourse on making LIFE decisions and wonder how you can make such decisions. Many people find it difficult to change their behavior or their outlook on life and often feel as if the harder they try, the harder it gets. Some have already gone through the process of deciding to make certain changes to their lives, but they quickly slide back into the same old habits. Some decide to study spiritual teachings or practice spiritual techniques, but after a short or long while, they feel as if nothing has really changed. Let me offer some thoughts on how to make LIFE decisions. I will be saying some of the same things I said in my latest discourse, but I will be saying them in a different way so as to hopefully help those who feel they do not yet have the full grasp on how to make life-changing decisions.

The first thing you need to understand is that you cannot make a LIFE decision with the outer mind and will. It must be a decision that comes from within, from the Conscious You itself. You cannot bring about a life decision with the outer will, you cannot force it, you cannot take heaven by force. However, neither can you bring about a

LIFE decision by passively waiting for it, thinking it will one day happen by itself. We might say that you cannot force a LIFE decision no matter how hard you try, but neither will it happen if you are not trying.

What I mean here is that a LIFE decision is a natural – even spontaneous – result of the right frame of mind, namely a frame of mind in which you have clarity. When you see how the ego has been hurting you, you will spontaneously make the LIFE decision to let go of a particular ego game. Imagine that you think you have been holding a rope in your hand, but you suddenly see that it is a snake. You don't have to reason about what to do; you simply let go of the snake. The key is to put yourself in a state of mind where you are receptive to the insights that can bring about a spontaneous decision. However, you don't have to simply wait passively for a clearer vision to happen. You can take active measures to bring it about, but it must be the right measures.

Knowing better

Master MORE is fond of saying: "If people knew better, they would do better." This is a true statement—when you recognize that "knowing better" does not refer to outer, intellectual knowledge but knowledge that has become internalized. In the last discourse I said that the real problem is that you have accepted a lower sense of identity based on a lack of true knowledge. When you internalize knowledge, that knowledge becomes part of your sense of identity and then expands your identity. When you accept this new identity, you will begin to act accordingly, meaning that you will effortlessly do better than you could do with your old sense of identity.

For example, virtually everyone has an outer knowledge that smoking is dangerous to their health. Those who still smoke have not internalized this knowledge. They do not truly know better because they have not fully understood how smoking affects them. They do not actually "see" that smoking is hurting themselves, and that is why they can keep smoking. Once you have an intuitive experience that shows you how smoking affects you, you will suddenly realize: "Why am I doing this?" At that point, it will be easy to stop because you realize that smoking is no longer compatible with the type of person you are.

Based on this, we can get a slightly different perspective on the master strategy of the ego. What the ego and the prince of this world are truly trying to do is to prevent you from knowing better. If you truly saw that you have an ego, that it is not the real you and that everything the ego does leads to suffering, you would instantly commit yourself to rising above the ego— thus making the master LIFE decision that puts you on the spiritual path. If you truly saw the nature and consequences of a particular ego game, you would instantly refuse to play that game, making an individual LIFE decision that would take you one step up the spiral staircase.

We can now see that the ego's survival depends on it remaining unknown to the Conscious You. The ego thrives in the shadows and in order to survive – or even expand its power – it must remain hidden. It now becomes clear that the ego will do anything in its power to prevent you from seeing the ego and seeing through its games. It wants you to keep thinking you are the ego rather than realizing that the Conscious You is separate from the ego. It wants to prevent you from recognizing the ego games and their consequences.

The ego has several layers of defenses aimed at preventing you from fully seeing it and its affect on your life. To illustrate this, let me go back to my example of an alcoholic. Few people consciously decide: "I'm gonna become an alcoholic." They slide into it gradually, often by using alcohol to dull the pain caused by a problem they cannot or will not solve. Dulling the pain instead of dealing with the problem causes more pain, and in order to avoid that, they drink some more, quickly sliding into a pattern that takes over their lives.

What is the first step towards recovery? Many people drink too much, which is plain for all to see—except themselves. They will deny that their drinking is a problem and refuse to acknowledge themselves as alcoholics. As any therapist can tell you, the first step towards recovery is the recognition that there is a problem. That is why it is so valuable when society recognizes a problem, perhaps by labeling it as a disease, and then focuses more attention on the problem and its consequences for individuals and society. Organizations such as AA have done an immense service by focusing attention on the problem of alcoholism and the potential for getting help. Unfortunately, Western civilization has not yet recognized the problem of the ego, but this will change within a decade or two.

The ego's first line of defense is to prevent you from even realizing that there is such a thing as an ego or seeing that it is the cause of your suffering. Most people are completely unaware of the ego and think their suffering is either normal or unavoidable. They have not realized that the ego is a problem and cannot even begin to overcome it. For many people this is simply because they have never been told about the ego in a way they could understand. For others it is because they are not willing to even consider the possibility that their suffering could be caused by something inside themselves. They want to keep seeing themselves as victims of outside forces so they have an excuse for not taking command of their lives.

After you recognize that there is a problem, the next step is to recognize that *you* have that problem. This is where the ego is often most successful in terms of fooling people. It is so easy to see the splinter in your brother's eye and so much harder to see the beam in your own eye. The ego is extremely skillful in making people think it is not their fault. Many spiritual people have attained an intellectual understanding of the ego, but they have not fully "seen" that they have an ego and how it runs their lives.

Once you recognize that there is a problem and that you are affected by that problem, you need to come to the recognition that if you are to overcome the problem, you are the one who must do something about it and you must begin now. The ego will do anything it can to make it seem like you can't or don't need to take action to overcome the ego. It is even possible for people to think that the ego is an external condition over which they have no control. This is much like an alcoholic who thinks he is the victim of a disease that cannot be cured but only held at bay.

Another area where the ego is often successful is in getting people to postpone – indefinitely – dealing with the ego. The ego is a master procrastinator and will seek to get you so occupied with other things that you never quite get the time to deal with the ego. Or it will get you to think you don't need to deal with the ego today—you can do it in the tomorrow that never comes.

After you recognize that the ego is a problem, that it affects you, that you have to deal with it and that you have to do so *now*, what could possibly go wrong? You have to understand what you are dealing with and how to best overcome it. This means understanding the nature and origin of the ego and seeing through the ego games. The latter is another area where the ego is often successful in fooling people. It is often quite difficult to identify a seemingly innocent habit as an ego game and actually see that you are trapped in that game. Human beings are very adaptable, which has the positive quality of allowing them to survive many different conditions. Adaptability can be used by the ego to make you tolerate ego-games. You have become so used to them that you think they are harmless or even normal. The good old argument that if everyone is doing it, it couldn't be wrong is still very effective for most people. It is a simple fact that if everyone is blinded by the ego, then everyone will indeed be wrong.

What is my purpose for listing the ways the ego is trying to prevent you from getting to the point of taking action and making a LIFE decision? Simply to make you aware of the areas where the ego will seek to hide so that you can begin to understand the mechanics of how the ego seeks to blind and pacify you. I hope you can begin to see that the ego was created because the Conscious You refused to be aware. The key to overcoming the ego is to take back awareness and increase your understanding. The ego truly has no actual power over you, and it can only influence you as long as you do not see what is happening. As you become aware of the ego and its games, you are well on your way to rising above it all. You must seek the right kind of awareness.

What to look for

There is outer knowledge and there is inner knowledge. There is intellectual knowledge and there is true understanding. There is the dualistic, relative "truth" of anti-christ and there is the undivided truth of Christ. As long as you look at life through the filter of the dualistic mind, the ego will always be able to hide from you. In order to expose the ego, you need to reach beyond the state of consciousness of the ego. You need to reach for vertical knowledge instead of intellectual knowledge. Some psychologists have great intellectual knowledge about the psyche, but they are no closer to seeing the ego in themselves. Some spiritual seekers have great intellectual knowledge about spiritual teachings, but they still have not understood the essential element of the path, namely that you must overcome the ego. Consider the following situation from the Bible:

> 3 And the scribes and Pharisees brought unto him a woman taken in adultery; and when they had set her in the midst,
> 4 They say unto him, Master, this woman was taken in adultery, in the very act.
> 5 Now Moses in the law commanded us, that such should be stoned: but what sayest thou?
> 6 This they said, tempting him, that they might have to accuse him. But Jesus stooped down, and with [his] finger wrote on the ground, [as though he heard them not].
> 7 So when they continued asking him, he lifted up himself, and said unto them, He that is without sin among you, let him first cast a stone at her.
> 8 And again he stooped down, and wrote on the ground.
> 9 And they which heard it, being convicted by their own conscience, went out one by one, beginning at the eldest, even unto the last: and Jesus was left alone, and the woman standing in the midst.
> (John, Chapter 8)

Here we have a group of people who were absolutely convinced that they were right, but in reality they were blinded by their egos. I, as the representative of the Christ mind – as the Living Christ – served to jolt them out of their spiritual blindness and make them look at the situation without the filter of the ego. They gained a new clarity and walked away from an inhumane act. I wish I could have been as successful in many other situations, but alas people were too blinded by their egos and unwilling to walk through that veil of illusions. Anyway, what you need in order to overcome your own ego is that kind of new perspective so you see what you could not see before.

Now consider the story of the Gordian Knot. An intricate knot was placed in an ancient temple and an oracle had prophesied: "He who can undo the Gordian knot will become ruler over all of Asia." Many people tried to untie the knot, but finally a young man named Alexander drew his sword and cut the knot in two. Alexander did not try to untie the ropes. He looked at the problem in a different way and found the only practical solution. He "undid" the knot as the oracle had said.

The moral of the story is that you cannot solve a problem while you are trapped in the same state of consciousness that created the problem. Your current problems were all created because you made Death decisions, decisions based on the dualistic logic of the mind of anti-christ presented by your ego. If you try to solve those problems with the same frame of mind, you will only dig an even deeper hole for yourself. Instead, you must do something different, bring a different element to replace the illusion.

This is illustrated in the old analogy that you cannot remove darkness from a room because it has no substance. No matter how much you analyze the darkness, you will still be in the dark. The only way out is to realize that darkness is not a substance in itself, but an absence of something. Once you bring what is missing, the darkness disappears. Likewise, the mind of anti-christ has no reality to it but is simply the absence of the reality of the Christ mind.

That is why Albert Einstein said: "If you keep doing the same thing and expect different results, you are insane." Most human beings are engaged in the insanity of trying to solve the problems created by the ego while still using the consciousness of the ego. It simply cannot be done. Zen Buddhism is known for using koans, which are short, often contradictory, statements designed to jolt the mind into looking at a situation in a different way. A koan is not meant to give you a specific piece of information or even understanding. It is actually meant to short-circuit the normal thinking patterns of the brain so that you suddenly step outside of your normal mental box. A koan is designed to help you realize that there is a state of consciousness above and beyond the dualistic state of mind that has become the normal state for most people. I often used similar statements because it was my goal to help people connect to the Christ mind. As I said:

> God is a Spirit: and they that worship him must worship him in spirit and in truth. (John 4:24)

The ego thinks entirely in a horizontal way, meaning that it simply cannot reach beyond a certain level. It is as if the ego is trapped in the basement of a house and cannot see that there is anything above it. My father's house has many mansions, and there is an entirely different way of thinking that is above the dualistic thinking of the ego. This is the kind of thinking that you need to be aware of, and you need to open your mind to receiving intuitive insights that will jolt your mind out of its own patterns.

Most people are not willing to think outside the box, and that is why their minds are closed most of the time. They want every new idea to conform to their present beliefs, to fit inside their current mental box. You can make the decision that you will be aware of the mind's tendency to close up and that you will counteract it. You can decide to put yourself in a receptive frame of mind where you are always open to a truth that your ego cannot see. You can decide that you are willing to look for the beam in your own eye and that you will be alert to your ego's attempts to make you focus your attention elsewhere. This is a state of listening grace and I talked about it when I said:

> He that hath ears to hear, let him hear. (Matthew 11:15)

> But blessed are your eyes, for they see: and your ears, for they hear. (Matthew 13:16)

> Verily I say unto you, Whosoever shall not receive the kingdom of God as a little child, he shall not enter therein. (Mark 10:15)

By becoming more aware of the need to reach beyond the ego's mental box, you will put your mind in a state of receptivity, and you will begin to receive the insights that will form the basis for LIFE decisions. Take note that this is not a passive state of mind. You are not simply waiting for the truth to find you. You are actively looking for the truth by studying anything that is available on the ego, on psychology and on spirituality. You are not studying to get intellectual, horizontal knowledge, you are studying to get intuitive breakthroughs, "Aha experiences," that give you vertical insights.

Always looking beyond duality

The master key here is to realize that you must always strive to increase your vision and discernment so you can look beyond the ego games. As we will see, there are several layers of ego games. In the beginning you cannot see through all of the ego's illusions so you will still be making dualistic decisions, but some of them will have less destructive consequences than others. This is not to say that dualistic decisions are necessarily bad. Some can be a step in the right direction, but you will not truly rise above a problem until you make a LIFE decision.

To use my previous example of alcoholism, there are many people who drink too much but who have not come to the recognition: "I'm an alcoholic and I need help!" Coming to this awareness is clearly a step in the right direction because it represents a higher level of awareness. Entering a treatment program or in other ways putting a stop to drinking will clearly be beneficial to the person. However, living the rest of your life with the sense of identity that "I'm an alcoholic" is not the highest possible outcome.

Coming to the awareness that "I'm an alcoholic" is not a LIFE decision. However, if you follow it up with expanding your spiritual understanding, you can come to the realization that you are a spiritual being. When you accept this new identity, you have made a LIFE decision. You have now allowed the old identity to die and a new identity has been born, according to which drinking is no longer an option. You are not even tempted to drink because it is incompatible with your new identity and world view.

Again, how can you come to the point where you can make such a LIFE decision? You must begin by expanding your awareness, which has two aspects:

• The Alpha aspect is to expand your understanding of the spiritual side of life, including that you are a spiritual being who has a unique mission on this planet. You understand the ego and see that you are more than the ego.

- The Omega aspect is that you understand why and how a certain pattern of behavior affects yourself and other people. You understand the ego games themselves.

Many people come to realize that certain habits have negative consequences, but they do not understand that they are ego games. They have to fight hard to overcome a habit, yet if you work on both aspects of expanding your understanding, it will become much easier for you to let go of the old way of thinking. The reason being that you will not actually feel you are giving up anything. Many people who stop drinking feel they have given up something that was pleasurable and they feel a loss or vacuum inside. Once you attain a higher spiritual understanding, you can overcome this illusion of loss.

You now have a new sense of identity instead of a vacuum, and you are not giving up anything. You are simply letting something old fall away as it is being replaced by something better. It is similar to what happened in your teen-age years when you one day realized: "I'm not a child anymore!" At that moment, you accepted a new identity, and it was now easy to give up playing with toys. You did not have to force yourself to stop playing with dolls or toy cars, you simply lost interest and focused your attention on a new type of toys that were suited to your new identity as a teenager.

I know some will say they would have been better off if they had stuck to their childhood toys, but the teenage stage was a necessary step on the path to adulthood. Eventually you gave up seeing yourself as a teenager and accepted yourself as an adult. You have already made a number of LIFE decisions that took you to a higher sense of identity. Making LIFE decisions is not something mysterious or out of this world; it is a normal part of life.

You simply need to become more aware of these kind of decisions and then focus your attention on taking the next step. You need to let the old identity as a "normal" adult fall away and accept a new identity as a spiritual being. When you do this, you will naturally stop doing what normal adults do and instead begin to do what spiritual beings do.

Opposition to progress

Many people feel like there is opposition to making a LIFE decision, like something is pulling them back into old patterns. Some people even experience making a LIFE decision but are still pulled back into old patterns. The reason is that there truly is a gravitational force that pulls you down the spiral staircase. This force has several components, and we will take a look at them next.

At the core of every ego game is an incorrect belief, meaning a belief that is based on the dualistic illusions of the mind of anti-christ rather than the reality of the mind of Christ. As long as this belief remains in your consciousness, it will pull on your mind, and it will literally pull you into patterns of thoughts, feelings and actions. You will not be free until you have overcome the incorrect belief. However, this can be complicated by the fact that a belief can have several layers. We might say that there is one deeper belief that is held in place or hidden by smaller beliefs, almost like smaller rocks holding a big boulder in place. Until you move the smaller rocks, you simply cannot get the boulder rolling. The material universe has four levels that correspond to the four levels of your mind:

- The identity level is where you have beliefs about who you are and how the world is.

•   The mental level is the level of thought and this is where you have beliefs about what you can and cannot do.

•   The emotional level is the level of feeling, which gives you the impetus to act. However, feelings can also be triggered by outer circumstances and prevent you from acting or get you to do something you really did not want to do. This is where you have beliefs about what you should and should not do.

•   The physical level is the level of the body and outer mind, and this is where you decide what physical actions to take. This is where you have beliefs about how your actions affect yourself and other people.

In most cases, an ego game will have components or beliefs on all four levels, and in order to fully escape the game, you must resolve them at all four levels.

As an example, let us go back to the alcoholic. At the conscious level, the person has the belief: "I'm not an alcoholic. I'm not drinking too much. I can handle this. I could stop any time." The physical level is where people usually experience consequences that can be difficult to deny. For example a person who is drinking might lose a job, destroy a relationship or be told by the doctor that if he doesn't stop drinking, he will be dead in six months. This might cause the person to abandon the belief I just described and cause him to stop drinking.

Obviously, this is a step in the right direction, but the person did not start drinking because of the belief that he is not an alcoholic and can stop any time. If he does not go beyond the level of the outer mind, the beliefs at the higher levels of the person's mind will still affect him and that is why he will have a life-long struggle with alcoholism. At the emotional level there might be a belief which says: "I should not be feeling this pain but since I am the victim of it, it is okay to dull the pain. I deserve a relief." Obviously, as long as that belief remains in the person's emotional body and as long as he feels pain, it will give him an emotional craving to drink and he must fight it daily.

At the level of the mental body, there might be a belief which says: "I can't solve this problem so I can't avoid feeling the pain of it. Since there is nothing I can do about it, my only option is to get some relief so I can deal with today." Again, this belief will continue to pull on the person's thoughts until it is removed. Finally, in the person's identity body might be the belief: "I'm just a human being and I'm worthless. Life has no purpose and there is really no point in me being here." This belief is the boulder, and if you could get it to move, it would pull the lower beliefs down with it.

It is quite possible that the Conscious You can step outside of your current situation, uncover the incorrect belief at the identity level and resolve it. Thereby, the lower beliefs will simply fall like dominoes. The problem here is that in order to do this, the Conscious You has to be able to pull back from your situation. You will have to look at the forest instead of the trees, and the ego will seek to lock your attention at one of the lower levels.

As long as a person is drinking too much, all of his attention is focused on the physical level. It is a matter of getting the next drink and avoiding the consequences of his drinking. It may be necessary for a person to stop the physical habit before his attention can be free to look beyond the physical level. Likewise, some people are so focused on the emotional level that they can never step back and realize their feelings are caused by their thoughts. Of course, some people are so focused on the mental and intellectual level that they do not realize their thoughts are simply the slaves of their sense of identity.

By seeking the kind of intuitive insights I talked about in the previous sections, you can ideally step back and uncover the incorrect belief at the identity level that is the cause of your problems. By pulling the plug in the bathtub, all the dirty water in the tub will run out. In many cases, it is too hard for people to free their minds from one of the lower levels. It may be necessary for you to first focus on overcoming an incorrect belief at the level of the conscious mind, at the emotional level or at the mental level. Only when you free your mind from its obsession with one of the lower levels, can you step back and look at the big picture.

The energy connection

As explained, everything is energy. The four levels of your mind form an energy field, and you are alive and conscious because there is a stream of energy flowing from your I AM Presence through your four lower "bodies." All of your mental processes make use of that light, and the light is inevitably "colored" by the beliefs you hold in the four levels of your mind. A belief that is based on the mind of anti-christ will lower the vibration of the light so that it cannot flow back up to your I AM Presence.

Part of this "misqualified" energy will accumulate in your personal energy field—often called your subconscious mind. Because this energy is electromagnetic energy, it exerts an electromagnetic force on your thoughts and emotions, pulling them into certain patterns. If you often respond to situations with anger, energy qualified with the vibration of anger will accumulate in your emotional body and this will pull you into responding with anger more easily. The more energy that has accumulated, the lower your anger threshold will be. If you have a lot of a certain type of misqualified energy in your personal field, this energy will have a twofold effect:

• The energy will act as a magnet that pulls your conscious awareness away from seeing the big picture. You become focused on the kind of actions, feelings or thoughts that correspond to the energy. You are not actually choosing your actions, feelings and thoughts because you are pulled into a pattern that is eating up your attention. The Conscious You will find it much more difficult to step back and say: "Why do I keep doing this?"

• The energy will form a veil that prevents the Conscious You from making contact with your Christ self, your spiritual teachers and your I AM presence. This also makes it harder for you to have an intuitive experience or see the underlying truth in a spiritual teaching you are reading.

In summary, the energy pulls your awareness into lower activities and prevents you from receiving the insights you need in order to know better. It now becomes obvious that you need to do something to get rid of this accumulated energy, and the most efficient way is to use a spiritual technique designed for this purpose. Obviously, the technique I will recommend is our decrees and invocations that are designed to both transform negative energy and help you resolve dualistic beliefs. [These tools are available on *www.transcendencetoolbox.com.*]

Quite frankly, there are very few people who could not benefit from using these tools as a preparation for making LIFE decisions. There are many people who have so much misqualified energy that they simply will not be able to make LIFE decisions until they have cleared out so much of it that they free their attention from the magnetic pull. Only then will they have enough self-awareness to see beyond the mental box created by their egos.

Another consequence of having misqualified energy in your personal field is that it creates a connection between your mind and the mass mind. Consider that you walk by a building that contains a huge electromagnet. Your body is not magnetic so you feel nothing. Now consider that your pockets are full of iron weights. You will now feel the pull of the magnet. If you have a lot of misqualified energy in your personal field, you will feel a pull from the mass consciousness, and this will make it much harder for you to make LIFE decisions. Again, the only way out is to transform the misqualified energy by using a spiritual technique. Then the prince of this world will come and have nothing in you whereby he can pull you into self-destructive patterns.

Before we leave the topic of something pulling you into old patterns, let me briefly mention habits. The subconscious mind functions much like a computer. Once a program has been created, it will keep running until you remove it from the computer's hard drive. You can make a LIFE decision that removes the false belief that created the program, but you still have certain grooves that exist in the subconscious mind. Once a trail is formed in a jungle, the animals will follow it. That makes the trail wider, meaning more animals will follow it. Likewise, a trail in your subconscious mind will cause your thoughts and feelings to follow certain patterns. The trail was established through repetition and it will require repetition to erase it.

Even after you make a LIFE decision, you will still have to erase the habit established after you accepted the old belief.

This will take some time and that is why you should be prepared to affirm a LIFE decision a number of times after you have made it. Some people have volunteered to help resolve patterns in the mass consciousness, and they might have to reaffirm certain LIFE decisions for a long time, even a lifetime. You should not be discouraged by this but simply keep affirming the decision whenever something pulls you back towards the old pattern.

The relationship between you and your beliefs

When you look at the world, you will see that some people are willing to die for their beliefs or they are willing to kill others in order to destroy what they see as a threat to their beliefs. Some of these people are even seen as heroes who take a stand, and some people even think I was willing to die for my beliefs. This is an incorrect understanding.

A belief is something that is expressed in words, and anything that is expressed in words has entered the realm of duality where it is subject to different interpretations. Here is an example of a belief: "My religion is the only true one and God wants all other religions destroyed so it is acceptable that I kill non-believers." In short, you should never be willing to die or kill for a belief.

You might indeed take a stand for a higher principle, and that is what I did by letting myself be crucified. However, I did not do this out of any self-centered motivation or attachment. I did it in an attempt to awaken others by showing them that their beliefs were contradictory. They claimed to believe in a religion that said: "Thou shalt not kill" yet they were ready to kill me in order to preserve their religion. How can you preserve a non-violent religion through violence? It is not my intention here to go into a complex philosophical discussion

so I am leaving certain things unexplained. My purpose here
is to show you the basic principle behind making LIFE decisions. The simple fact is that you have become blinded by the
dualistic illusions of the ego, and you no longer see Christ
truth. Your vision of truth is being blocked by your current
beliefs. In order to attain the vision of Christ – which makes
it natural and effortless to make a LIFE decision – you must
be willing to look beyond your current beliefs. You cannot do
this as long as you are attached to those beliefs. Being willing
to kill or die for your beliefs is simply the extreme form of such
attachment.

There are many people who will notice that as they read
these ego discourses, they have a certain uneasiness somewhere in their minds. If you look closer, you will see that there
is a reluctance to have your current beliefs exposed as being
erroneous. There can even be a fear that if your beliefs are
exposed as errors, something bad will happen or you will suf-
fer a loss. What will be left if you lose your beliefs?

I am in no way finding fault with people who feel this way,
I am simply pointing out that as long as you have these feelings, you will make the spiritual path much more difficult for
yourself than it needs to be. I have a desire to see all sincere
seekers walk the path as quickly and as painlessly as possible.
In order to do that, you only have to shift your perspective
on life a little bit. You have to turn the dial of consciousness
slightly so that you look at beliefs in a different way.

What is the new perspective? As long as you have any kind
of attachment to your current beliefs, it will cause you pain to
let go of those beliefs. For each step you take on the spiritual
path, you must let go of an erroneous belief, meaning that each
step will cause you pain. When you are reluctant to let go of an
erroneous belief, it is because there is a part of you that is identifying itself with that belief. That part is, of course, the ego. It

does not want you to grow and is using your present beliefs to hold back your growth.

What is the hidden message that the ego is giving you? It is that you should not let go of a particular belief because there is nothing beyond it—it is infallible. If you allow your ego to make you attached to your beliefs, you are essentially refusing to expand your understanding and acquire the broader perspective that will bring about a LIFE decision. Am I saying that you need to let go of all your beliefs? Not necessarily, but I am saying that you need to *be willing* to let go of all your beliefs. If there is a belief that you are not willing to question, then that unwillingness comes from an attachment and an attachment can only come from the ego.

How do you escape this trap? There literally is only one way. The Conscious You must come to the realization that you are more than your beliefs! As I have explained, the Conscious You is an individualization of God's Being and God is clearly beyond any belief in this world. God is the Spirit of Truth and that is why you must worship him in Spirit and in truth—instead of worshiping him through dualistic beliefs and earthly doctrines. God's Spirit is beyond any belief that can be put into words. The trick is, of course, that only the Conscious You can experience the Spirit of Truth whereas the ego can never do so.

If you can make that shift in consciousness, you can realize that the real you can never lose anything by letting go of an erroneous belief. How could you lose by letting go of a belief that limits and imprisons you in a false sense of identity that causes constant suffering? Only the ego can lose when you let go of a false belief so the ego can no longer control you.

When you know you are more than your beliefs, you can quickly overcome all fear of taking a look at your beliefs and all fear of what will happen if a dearly held belief is exposed as erroneous. Instead of resisting the process of having your erroneous beliefs exposed, you actively seek out such exposure. Not all at once so you lose your bearings, but you commit yourself to an ongoing process of gradually exposing every wrong belief that has ever entered your mind. Once you see such a belief, you can simply let it go as effortlessly as you let go of a snake. You will then begin to make spontaneous LIFE decisions and that is when your progress on the path will accelerate beyond your present expectations.

Being teachable

As one last thought on how to get yourself in a state of mind where LIFE decisions begin to happen spontaneously, ask yourself the following questions: "Am I teachable? Am I willing to follow a true spiritual teacher who exposes my false beliefs? Or would I rather follow a false teacher who tells me what I (in reality, your ego) want to hear?"

These are the quintessential questions that separate the true spiritual seekers from those who might claim to be very spiritual or religious but who have not yet understood what the path is about or have not made a commitment to their own growth. This literally separates the sheep from the goats.

The situation is undeniable. In order to make progress on the spiritual path – in order to take the next step up the spiral staircase – you must overcome the false belief that caused you to descend to your current step. If you could see the fallacy of that illusion, you would not have descended that step or you would already have gone back up. What is blocking your progress is that there is something you cannot see, and as long as you cannot see it, you will remain trapped.

The key to breaking the gridlock is that you must receive the crucial insight that allows you to expose your current belief as false and replace it with the truth that makes you free. Where is that insight going to come from? It cannot come from inside your own mind, inside your current mental box. If the insight you need was inside the box, you would already have found it. Take another look at my statement:

> And why beholdest thou the mote that is in thy broth-
> er's eye, but perceivest not the beam that is in thine own
> eye? (Luke 6:41)

Why is it so easy for people to see what is going on in other people's lives and so hard to see the same problem in their own lives? Because when you are inside the mental box created by the ego, you cannot see your situation as clearly as when you look at it from the outside. The insight you need must come from a source that is outside your mind and above the level of duality. That source is a spiritual teacher.

This does not mean that you have to make a direct or conscious contact with a being in the spiritual realm. As Master MORE says: "If the teacher be an ant, heed him." The meaning is that the teacher often appears in an unexpected or humble disguise. The teacher might be a book or it might be another person who tells you what you cannot see on your own. As I have already mentioned, when the student is ready, the teacher will appear. There is always a teacher with you who can give you exactly what you need in order to take the next step on your path. The big question is whether you can recognize the teacher and whether you are willing to heed the message?

What you can do right now is to make a commitment that you will always look for the teacher. You will allow the teacher to tell you what you cannot see and what your ego does not want you to see. You will look for a true teacher who challenges your illusions, instead of a false teacher who makes you comfortable in your illusions. You can decide that you will strive to be teachable for the rest of your life, always looking for the teacher who can take you to a higher level. You can decide that you will have ears to hear and eyes to see.

The path is an ongoing process

There are many people who fall prey to the ego's tendency to look for an automatic or guaranteed salvation, as I explained in earlier discourses. They think there is some kind of ultimate teaching, information or insight and once they have found it, they will be home free. They think one magical decision will whisk them to the top of the spiral staircase.

As long as you are in embodiment, you will be dealing with the mind of anti-christ. You can free yourself from most of your own ego, but you will still be exposed to the mass consciousness from without. It is essential for you to go into a frame of mind in which you see the path as an ongoing process. Instead of looking for some final solution, you look forward to receiving progressively higher insights for the rest of your lifetime.

When you do this, you are no longer looking for some ultimate teaching, which means the ego cannot make you believe you have now found an infallible truth and you can stop looking. The ego cannot make you stop at a certain step, causing you to think you do not have to take the next step. In the last discourse I said that you must not allow the ego to supply the information upon which you base your decisions. The reason is that if you do so, the ego will make you think you do not have to go further because you are saved where you are. It will make you think your current step is the last step you need to take.

The web of illusions spun by the ego is very subtle, and you should consider that the path has several levels. Instead of allowing the ego to make you feel comfortable at your current level, you should always be looking beyond it. There are levels of ego games, and you need to keep going until you reach the highest level and overcome your false sense of identity. Understanding this will serve to encourage you because you will realize that you have risen above the lowest level of ego games.

There is a subtle difference that you need to ponder. The ego will try to make you feel comfortable with your current beliefs so you do not move on. Fighting this tendency does not mean you have to live the rest of your life in a state of dissatisfaction or lack. Once you realize you are more than your beliefs, letting go of an old belief does not cause you pain. It causes you to feel freer, and that gives rise to joy. You can enjoy the journey without falling into the trap of becoming so comfortable that you stop the progress. When you reach that childlike innocence, you can approach the spiritual path with the same excitement as a child who has discovered a wonderful new playground to explore. At that point, you have entered the kingdom of Heaven even though you have not yet reached the top of the spiral staircase.

Let me return to my statement that you cannot bring about a LIFE decision no matter how hard you try but that it will not happen if you are not trying. We now see that as long as you try by using the mind of anti-christ, you cannot attain the Christ vision that is the foundation for a LIFE decision. If you just passively wait for a decision to happen, you will get nowhere. The key is that there is a middle way between trying with the human mind and doing nothing.

That narrow way is to put yourself in a frame of mind where you are seeking first the kingdom of God – the Christ vision – and then letting all other things – including LIFE decisions – be added onto you spontaneously. It is a state of graceful expectancy where you make yourself – your mind – a chalice and allow God's truth to flow into it and replace the darkness.

Upholding the ego's illusions is what requires a constant struggle. Attaining Christ truth only requires you to stop struggling. That is the true meaning of having the innocent mind of a child. You separate yourself from the ego's attempt to control everything and instead – to use another of Master MORE's expressions – you TRY by letting Theos Rule You. You allow God within you to be the doer instead of letting the ego be the doer.

> I can of mine own self do nothing: as I hear, I judge: and my judgment is just; because I seek not mine own will, but the will of the Father which hath sent me. (John 5:30)

> Believest thou not that I am in the Father, and the Father in me? the words that I speak unto you I speak not of myself: but the Father that dwelleth in me, he doeth the works. (John 14:10)

Try to read those two statements with the feeling that you are the Christ speaking them. Then pay attention to how your ego will resist the message.

3 | UNDERSTANDING THE NORM OF THE EGO

There are some ego games that are very specific, and they are relatively easy to expose when they are out-played in specific situations. There are other ego games that are more general, and they can be difficult to expose because they apply in many different situations, even in all situations. These general ego games often set the stage for the specific ego games, and they can impair your ability to see through and rise above the specific games. I will therefore begin by talking about one of the general ego games.

In order to help you understand this game, let us summarize what I have explained in the previous couple of discourses:

- The ego wants to blind you to the existence of a higher reality that is beyond the dualistic thinking of the ego.

- Once you are blinded by that illusion, the ego wants to keep you there indefinitely.

• The ego wants you to go where it wants you to go without you realizing what is happening. It wants to take you down the staircase of life so gradually that you don't notice the descent.

• If you refuse to go further down, the ego wants to keep you standing still at your present level. Even after you start climbing back up, the ego seeks to stop your growth at any level.

• It takes a distinct decision to stand up and start walking back up the staircase of life. The ego will do anything to prevent you from making such a LIFE decision.

What is the ego's primary weapon in attempting to prevent you from making LIFE decisions and taking the next step up the staircase of life? It is that the ego seeks to make you accept a norm, a definition of what is considered normal behavior. The ego will then project into your conscious mind that as long as you stay within what it has defined as normal, there is no reason for you to do anything out of the ordinary, such as making a LIFE decision and taking a distinct step up the staircase. The ego wants you to believe that sliding down the staircase or standing still is normal behavior whereas taking a step up the staircase is abnormal and unnecessary, dangerous, forbidden or impossible. The ego's message is: "Don't rock the boat—just keep doing what you have been doing and what everybody else is doing."

In this endeavor, the ego has a major ally, namely what some psychologists call the collective unconscious. We might also call it the mass consciousness or the planetary ego. When you look at society, you will see that many people live their entire lives within the norms of their particular society, blindly following the standards for normal behavior in anything from religion to fashion trends.

Throughout history, you will see that many societies have imposed various penalties for going beyond their norms. This can be drastic measures, such as being killed, deported, imprisoned or herded into railroad cars and taken off to a concentration camp. Or it can be less dramatic – and thus harder to expose – methods ranging from family and social pressure to simply not teaching people that there is a different way to look at life.

Once a society has created a state in which most people fear to go against or question the norm, that society has become rigid. There is little possibility of an internal change, which is why such societies often enter a downward slide that leads to their collapse, either through internal factors or an external enemy that conquers them. The Roman empire is a prime example, but many others litter the pages of history.

Historically speaking, very few societies have had norms that made it acceptable behavior to follow the spiritual path. Most societies have discouraged people from doing so—even – or perhaps especially – religious societies. That is why I was opposed, pressured and attacked from all sides when I started expressing my Christhood. All sincere spiritual seekers should expect that they will have to go beyond the norms of their society in order to pursue the spiritual path to its full extent. A spiritual seeker might as well accept the fact that spiritual growth is currently not seen as normal by any Western society. Once you expect to be abnormal – with whatever that entails in your particular environment – you are not as susceptible to your ego's subtle attempts to make you stay within the norm—stay within the fold.

Beyond your society, you also need to be aware of the inner pressure created by your ego itself. Your personal norm is clearly affected by the environment in which you grew up, but it also has its own personal characteristics that your ego has carefully created over many lifetimes. These are designed to keep you following what your ego has defined as normal, and a spiritual seeker must be wiling to examine his or her norms. No one ever has been successful on the spiritual path without examining and questioning – and then transcending – his or her personal norms as well as the external norm of the environment. For a spiritual seeker, going beyond the norm should be considered normal behavior.

The carrot and the stick

The concept of a norm implies a median value, a sort of average. But a median exists only in relation to two extremes, as an average is found somewhere between a high and a low. The ego seeks to define its norm by setting up a high and a low:

• The carrot is the highest you can attain, the wildest dream, your ultimate sense of happiness—according to the ego. Because the ego cannot see beyond the duality consciousness, it will define this high based on its own limited vision. Or it will define the way to attain this ultimate state based on its illusions. For example, many spiritual people have a somewhat correct vision in terms of thinking the ultimate goal of life is an exalted state in the spiritual realm. Their egos often manage to make them believe in the automatic path to that goal, as I explained in previous discourses. One obvious example is the belief that if you verbally confess Jesus Christ to be your Lord and Savior, then I will automatically take upon myself all of your sins and take you to heaven.

• The stick is your greatest fears, the vision of the worst that could possibly happen to you. Again, the ego will define this based on its own illusions, and there will always be a clear element of irrationality. All fear is irrational, for when you truly experience the reality of God, truth will set you free from all fear.

In reality, the ego's norm is a mental prison that is meant to keep you within the boundaries where your ego feels it can control you. The ego presents the norm as a safe zone that will guarantee that you attain your highest dream while keeping you safe from your worst fears. To use my previous example, as long as you believe Jesus will save you, you will be saved. As long as you do not question the doctrine of the vicarious atonement, you will avoid burning in hell.

The conclusion is simple. As long as you do not question the norm, including the carrot and the stick, you will stay within the mental box defined by your ego and no spiritual growth is possible. You will not begin to grow spiritually until you begin to question your ego's norm. The ego, of course, will do anything it can think of to make you believe questioning the norm is dangerous, and you must be prepared to question the reasons for why you should not question the norm.

As I said, all fear is irrational, and all irrationality can be removed through proper understanding. The very key to any kind of progress is to seek understanding. As the Bible itself puts it: "With all thy getting, get understanding." This is also why I often talked about those who have "ears to hear" or "eyes to see." It is why I told people that if they seek, they shall find, if they ask, they shall receive and if they knock, the door shall be opened unto them. I know the fear of questioning the norm is very persuasive so let me attempt to give you the clarity that will empower you to conquer it.

Why it is dangerous not to question the norm

As an example, I will use traditional Christian terminology. Most Christian churches would agree that you need to be saved because you have sinned. Why do you have the option to sin, why didn't God simply create you without that option so that there would be no question about whether or not you would be saved?

Most churches would also agree that you have to do something in order to be saved—you have to make certain choices. They often disagree on what you have to do, but that is not important in this context. The very fact that you are not automatically saved and that you have to do something in order to be saved shows that God gave you free will. Because you have free will, you can choose to go against God's law – thereby sinning and jeopardizing your salvation – or you can choose to align yourself with God's law and be saved.

The very fact that God gave you free will shows that while God wants you to enter his kingdom, he does not want to force you to do so. If he was a forceful God, he would have created you without the option to sin so that you would automatically be in God's kingdom. The logical conclusion is that God did not create you as a robot, but wants you to enter the kingdom out of your own free-will choosing.

What will it take for you to voluntarily enter God's kingdom? It will take that you understand that entering God's kingdom is what you really want, and doing what it takes to enter is in your own best interest. You must overcome any sense of fear, the sense that you are somehow forced to be saved because otherwise you will end up in a terrible place. You must overcome any sense of obligation, the sense that you should give up your earthly pleasures in order to enter heaven—which really is the subtle sense that being saved is a loss of earthly things.

Entering God's kingdom must be a completely free choice, and you can make a free choice only when you have the full understanding of what is involved in the choice. You must be able to see why choosing God's kingdom over an earthly kingdom is enlightened self-interest. You must see that you do not lose anything but gain something that is infinitely more valuable than anything you have on earth. If you do not have this full understanding, you simply cannot make a free choice. A choice that is based on even partial ignorance can never be a free choice.

The conclusion is clear. God wants you to make a free choice, which is why he gave you free will. God knows that when you have the full understanding of reality, you will lovingly choose God's kingdom over anything on earth. God wants you to have the full understanding of reality. God has nothing to hide and is not seeking to hide anything from you. It can only be the forces who seek to keep you out of God's kingdom that want to prevent you from having full understanding.

It is the ego and the prince of this world who are seeking to keep you in ignorance by making you believe that asking certain questions is dangerous. These forces have often used religion to stop people from asking questions, yet in this age it is time people rise above that intimidation and demand the full truth about their relationship with God. The reality is that God never seeks to discourage you from discovering the truth that will make you free. When you encounter any inner or outer resistance to your growth in understanding, you know the ego and the prince of this world are at work. Be willing to question the norm, be willing to transcend the norm, be willing to be more than the norm tells you that you can or are allowed to be.

The norm is an uneven standard

For the vast majority of human beings, the norm set by their egos is to not go beyond what is considered normal behavior in their society. Obviously, various cultures and societies have different standards for what is considered normal so the norms created in different parts of the world can vary greatly. They all say pretty much the same thing, namely that you should not do anything extraordinary. Just be an ordinary human being and you will reach whatever goal is defined. For example, just be an ordinary Christian and follow the doctrines of your church and then you will be saved.

Most people are happy to live what might be called "ordinary" lives by following the standard for what is considered normal. In every society there are people who cannot be satisfied by being normal, and they long for something extraordinary in their lives. They often engage in a sincere striving for excellence and seek to rise above "ordinary" people in a variety of ways.

Unfortunately, most of these people get trapped in another ego game, namely that of competing with others. Although their striving for excellence could potentially lead them to make progress on the spiritual path, as long as they are caught in the game of comparison, they are not truly rising above the ego. The ego loves to feel superior to others so for these people, their egos have simply defined a different norm. This norm says that instead of blending into the crowd, these people's norm is to stand out from the crowd. It is normal for them to be better than others.

In its extreme form, this can make people believe that they belong to a separate category of people, a higher class, that is inherently above the masses. For these people, superiority has become the norm, and their lives are eaten up by a quest to prove this superiority by any means, be it power, intelligence, education, sports, money, beauty or whatever else might be valued in their society.

Obviously, being involved with a spiritual teaching or movement is not above being used by the ego to create the sense of superiority. Many spiritual people have been trapped in pursuing a goal defined by their egos, often set up as the guaranteed path to salvation. As long as you follow the outer rules set by this or that spiritual organization, you will rise above others and be more spiritual—says the ego.

The vast majority of the spiritual organizations found on this planet have norms – sometimes clearly defined and sometimes unspoken or vague – that are partially or fully defined by the egos of the leaders and members of the organization. The ego has simply managed to make such people accept its norm for what it means to be a spiritual person.

Behind all norms is an underlying message, namely that it is never normal for you to go beyond being human—as defined by the consciousness of duality. The ego will let you rise however high you want, as long as you stay within the dualistic game of comparing yourself to others or to an outer standard. What the ego does not want to see is that you begin to attain union with your I AM Presence so that you begin to strive to be – here on earth – an extension of the Being you already are in the spiritual realm.

The ego knows that once you begin to know your spiritual being, you will see beyond any earthly standard and you will want MORE than the earth – or the ego – can offer. You will begin to become non-attached to the goals and norms defined by the ego, and this will gradually empower you to take command over your own mind and being. You can then follow the original call for all co-creators, namely to multiply and have dominion over the earth. Any norm defined by the ego has as its underlying goal to prevent you from attaining this non-dualistic approach to life. The ego will let you be any kind of human being you want to be, but it does not want you to be here below all that you are Above.

The norm, an ever-moving target

It is essential for spiritual seekers to realize that the ego's norm is not a fixed entity. As you grow on the spiritual path, your ego will adapt to your new beliefs, your new world view. Obviously, the ego would prefer to keep you away from the spiritual path and keep you trapped in the materialistic ego games that I will describe in coming discourses. If it cannot do so, it will simply change its norm to incorporate your spiritual beliefs while distorting them in subtle ways so that you still stay within the borders of being a human being.

I have already described the ego's attempt to create the illusion of an automatic salvation, and it is essential for all spiritual seekers to consider whether they have been trapped by their ego's attempt to set up a norm that appeases their spiritual beliefs while preventing any serious spiritual growth. The reality is that as long as you have any ego left, it will attempt to adapt its norm, including the stick and the carrot, to your present level of consciousness. The purpose is always to prevent you from going beyond your current state of consciousness. That is why it is so important for a spiritual seeker to realize that you can never stand still. Still-stand means that the ego will catch up to you, and when it does, it will create a new norm which makes it seem as if your current level on the spiritual path is all that is needed or possible. You should feel comfortable staying where you are and forget about going higher.

Be aware that the higher you climb on the path, the more subtle your ego becomes. As you educate yourself in spiritual concepts, you are also educating your ego, and it will use this education to create a norm that is very persuasive. This norm will play on all of your spiritual beliefs and it might contain much truth. Yet there is always that slight distortion which seeks to prevent you from transcending your current state of consciousness.

That is why you can never stand still, never allow yourself to become too comfortable. If you will take an honest look at spiritual organizations, you will see that there is a distinct pattern. Many members start out by eagerly following whatever path if offered in the organization. They apply themselves fully and often make great progress. As they climb the ranks of the outer organization, they gradually become more concerned about their outer positions than their inner progress.

They now seek to defend their positions rather than transcending them, and this is the hallmark of the ego. It is a sure sign that they have now accepted a new norm that reinforces the belief that they are very spiritual because they live up to outer characteristics defined by the dualistic vision of the ego. Many spiritual organizations have been perverted by this process and have lost their original transformative qualities. Instead, they now seek to trap people at a certain level and prevent them from going beyond the norm – overt or hidden – defined by the organization.

Questioning the norm

The effect of the norm is to get you to "do nothing" – or rather to continue to do the same thing – while feeling that you do not need to change yourself or any aspect of your life. That is why so many people only have a spiritual awakening when they experience a major crisis in their lives. Only when some outside event shatters their sense that everything is normal, that everything is okay, do they wake up and acknowledge that something needs to change.

Consider how many people are moving very gradually toward such a crisis, and everyone around them can see where they are going, but they cannot see it themselves. They cannot see it because so far nothing has disturbed the norm, the sense that they are okay and that nothing bad will happen as long as they keep doing what they are doing. The more blinded people are by the norms of their egos, the more severe the crisis that is needed in order to wake them up and make them willing to change.

It is always sad for a spiritual seeker to see how people move toward a crisis while ignoring all of the warning signals. They simply bury their heads in the sand and refuse to heed the people or events that are meant to signal that it is time to change course. As a spiritual teacher, I would very much wish that all sincere seekers would avoid this trap, but the only way to do so is to become aware of the ego's norm and be willing to question it.

The basic fact is that the ego's norm is always designed to prevent you from going beyond a certain level. You simply cannot go beyond that level until you see what is holding you back, namely a norm created by the dualistic mind. It is essential for all spiritual seekers to be aware of the existence of a norm and to always remain open to questioning it. This involves questioning all elements of the norm, including the high, the low and the median:

- **The Median.** It might be normal for most people to behave or believe a certain way, but that is not to say it is normal for spiritual seekers. If you truly understand the spiritual path, your goal should be to transcend yourself so this is the evaluation you need to apply. Will the norms I have in certain areas help me grow spiritually, or will they tie me to a certain level, a level that might be comfortable but does not lead to growth? You should also be aware that there is always a temptation to become comfortable at any level of the spiritual path. If you feel yourself becoming comfortable and start to think you do not need to go higher or that you can keep doing the same thing, then be alert and start questioning the norm that gives rise to such thoughts and feelings. Self-transcendence means that you cannot keep doing or believing the same thing for an indefinite period of time. There will come a time when it is necessary to make a LIFE decision and rise to an entirely new level.

• **The high.** Question your highest dreams or vision and be willing to go within and seek an even higher vision from your Christ self. Be aware that your ego can never truly understand the spiritual path so it cannot define the highest possible goal for you. That goal is already defined in your divine plan, and you only need to uncover it. In order to do so, you need to look beyond the limited vision of the ego. You also need to question the way the ego defines for reaching your/its goals. The ego can never understand self-transcendence so it will tend to come up with outer criteria for reaching whatever goals you have. Be willing to look beyond them. Study spiritual teachings and ask for direction from your Christ self so that you can refine your vision of how to reach your goals. Above all, always be willing to reach for more, for a higher vision than you have right now.

• **The low.** Be willing to realize that all fear springs from an illusion. The crippling effect of fear is that it makes you afraid to look at what you fear, and therefore you cannot discover that your fear is based on an illusion. Once you take a look, you see the irrationality of fear, and that is the first step to leaving it behind. Ask yourself: "What is the worst thing that could happen? Would that prevent me from learning my lessons and transcending myself?" When you begin to look beyond the ego's norms, you realize that the true goal of life is for you to grow spiritually, which means you have the potential to learn from every situation. Many people have grown tremendously from the worst tragedies. This is not to say you should long for a tragedy, but that you should realize that even if the worst happened, it would not mean the end of your spiritual growth. Once you begin to consider that even if the worst fears of your ego came to pass, it would only accelerate your growth, you begin to truly overcome the paralyzing effect of the ego's fears. Your Conscious You has no fear. Only the ego has fears so once you start separating yourself from the ego, you will no longer be overwhelmed by its fears, for you see how irrational and paranoid they are.

Why have I chosen to talk about this norm game before I talk about more specific ego games? Because for each of the specific ego games, there is a norm game. When you are caught in a specific ego game, you think the game is normal behavior, and you simply cannot see that there is anything wrong with it. You cannot see how it limits or even hurts yourself, let alone other people. You simply cannot see the beam in your own eye, and you obviously cannot start removing it.

Before you can even begin to see through a specific ego game, you must overcome the illusion that playing this game is normal behavior. You must realize that even if it is normal behavior for most human beings, it is not normal for a spiritual seeker, a person who wants spiritual freedom. You must realize that playing the game takes away your freedom, and this empowers you to start separating yourself from that specific game, eventually leaving it behind for good. The crucial point for overcoming any ego game is to have a moment of truth where you see what you are doing, see that it is an ego game and then have the spontaneous decision: "I can't keep doing this anymore, I want to come up higher."

In the beginning, such a moment of truth can be a shock to you because you are still so identified with the ego. It can cause you some emotional pain and hurt pride to realize that you are trapped in an ego game. As you begin to separate yourself from the ego, the shock will be less and less, until you can discover an ego game without feeling any sense of shock or pain. You simply see it for what it is and let it go, as easily as you throw away a pair of old pants that are worn out.

By building this momentum of seeing and letting go of ego games, you will make it easier for yourself to walk the path. In order to encourage this process, I will go on to talk about some of the most materialistic ego games, games that most spiritual seekers have moved beyond. I hope to help you see that you have already built a momentum on overcoming ego games. You simply need to become aware of this so you can apply it to the ego games you have not yet seen whereby you can overcome them without pain. The spiritual path is not a painful process, but a joyful process of letting go of what limits you so that you can experience greater freedom.

❧

The ego was born
from separation,
and it is incapable of
seeing beyond it
or even questioning it.

❧

4 | DEFINING EGO GAMES

In this book I will focus on what I call ego games and in the following book I will focus on what I call ego dramas. The distinction between the two is somewhat artificial because the ego often uses ego dramas to justify ego games, and it uses ego games to create ego dramas. For many people the two are intertwined in a very tangled web. My reason for making the distinction is to describe two levels of how you rise above the ego, namely the personal and the supra-personal level.

An ego game is directly related to you and what you do as an individual whereas an ego drama relates to what you do in relation to some greater – seemingly impersonal – consideration. We might say that an ego game is what people normally see as egotistical behavior, namely what revolves around your personal desires or needs. An ego drama goes beyond your personal level and relates to a greater cause. A drama is something you pretend to do for others or even for God, yet it is simply a camouflaged offspring of the ego. An ego game is often obvious selfish behavior whereas an ego drama is selfish behavior camouflaged as unselfish behavior. An ego game is what you do in relation to other people who are also focused on themselves. An ego drama is what you do in relation to a greater cause, even to God or to other people who are also pretending that their selfish behavior serves an altruistic cause.

Let me make this less abstract through a concrete example. Throughout history and even today you can find many people who have taken great personal pride in being good warriors or soldiers. They enjoy having a weapon and the training and skills for how to use it better than others. They take pride in going into combat and being able to kill the enemy. These are often the people who serve as soldiers or lower ranking officers in an army. They see themselves as being soldiers who do not make the decision to go to war and do not necessarily need a justification for doing so. They will fight any enemy that their leaders command them to fight because they enjoy the fighting.

You will also see that throughout history there have been an elite of people who rarely go to war themselves but who either make the decision to go to war or who command the soldiers from relative safety behind the front lines. There are cases where leaders have decided to go to war out of purely personal motives. As an example, consider the many times where groups of people or even armies have attacked others purely for plunder. Examples are the Vikings and the Huns who had no motive other than enriching themselves.

Beyond this you will see that in many cases nations have gone to war with what they saw as a higher motive or justification. An example is the Crusades where many people who enjoyed being warriors found a justification for ignoring their religious teachings about not killing under the pretense of liberating Jerusalem for the only true faith. The Muslims who fought the crusaders likewise felt justified in killing in the name of their God. There are those who are warriors and who take pride in being better in combat than others. They kill, but they need no particular justification for doing so. They do not necessarily enjoy killing, but they have accepted it as part of being a warrior and they often barely reflect upon it. This is an ego game. These people are clearly focused on themselves and doing what they want to do. They are not actually reflecting on whether killing is right or wrong. If you are a warrior, you kill your opponents as a lion kills its prey.

Then there are those who see themselves as leaders who are serving some greater cause. These people rarely if ever do the actual killing, and the main reason is that they have actually come to the realization that killing is not right. In many cases such leaders would find it very difficult to directly kill another human being, yet these same leaders find it relatively easy to make decisions that result in the killing of millions of people. How can you explain that a person can know that personally killing others is wrong but can still justify decisions that lead to the killing of millions of people? It is because these people have risen above the ego games but are now trapped in the ego dramas. They have used some philosophy to define that killing certain groups of people is necessary for a greater cause.

The first group of people are in a sense honest and simply do what they want to do. The second group are dishonest because they pretend that what they do is not something they want to do but something they are doing for a greater cause— or because circumstances are forcing them to do so. In reality, those trapped in ego dramas are still doing what they want to do, but they need a justification that this is not ego-based behavior but is sanctioned by a greater authority, such as fate, necessity or God.

This is why I called the Jewish religious leaders hypocrites and accused them of putting burdens upon the people that they were not willing to bear.

The levels of spiritual growth

The importance of the distinction becomes clear when you consider that the spiritual path has levels. In the previous book [*Freedom From Ego Illusions*] we discussed the fact that it is possible for a human being to be at 144 different levels of consciousness. The spiritual path can be described as a process where you rise towards the 144th level until you are ready to leave the earth behind permanently and ascend.

We described that there are three main levels of the spiritual path, namely from the first to the 48th level, from the 48th to the 96th level and from the 96th to the 144th level. A new lifestream will take embodiment on earth at the 48th level and this lifestream has not yet created an ego. In an ideal scenario, it is possible for a lifestream to maintain its contact with its spiritual teacher and work its way up towards the 144th level without ever going into the consciousness of separation and duality. The earth is not an ideal scenario so all people currently in embodiment did at some point create an ego.

There are two main reasons for creating an ego and they relate to the two main purposes for which the Conscious You descended into embodiment:

• The Conscious You wanted to experience the material world from the inside.

• The Conscious You wanted to help co-create the world from the inside.

When a lifestream is climbing from the 48th to the 96th level it is going through the seven spiritual rays, learning to use its co-creative powers through the qualities of each ray [For more about this, see *The Power of Self*.]. There is a temptation related to each level, namely that you can decide that you want the experience of using your co-creative abilities as a separate being. For example, the first ray is the ray of power and some lifestreams decide that they want the experience of being able to express personal power. This might cause them to create an ego that makes them see themselves as warriors who have the ultimate power to defeat an opponent in hand-to-hand combat. Others might have taken the initiations of the second ray of wisdom and decide they want to experience what it is like to be smarter than others intellectually. The colleges and scientific institutions of the world are full of such lifestreams.

We might say that between the 48th and the 96th level you are raising yourself as an individual being, seeking to expand your individual abilities. Your temptation is to avoid going into the ego games and if you have done so, your task is to rise above these games. When you rise above the 96th level, you start using your co-creative abilities for the good of others, even the All. This is when you must face the more subtle temptations represented by the desire to work for the good of the whole by forcing other individuals. This is what gives rise to the ego dramas, namely that you use some greater cause to justify what is truly ego-based behavior. As I hope you can see, the ego dramas are far more subtle and difficult to expose than the ego games. However, we will leave the subtlety of the ego dramas for the following book and here we will focus on the ego games.

Quite frankly, many spiritual seekers have risen above the most primitive or obvious ego games. Yet do not let your ego talk you into believing that you can skip this book or ignore its points. An ego drama is often a disguised ego game, and until you have fully seen the ego game at the personal level, it can be virtually impossible to expose the fallacy of the corresponding ego drama.

Realizing that you have risen above the more primitive ego games should be a source of encouragement because you can realize that you can surely rise above the rest as well. Take care to realize that rising above the more obvious and primitive behaviors related to an ego game does not necessarily mean you have completely risen above it. As mentioned in the previous book, it is quite possible for the ego to use a spiritual teaching to camouflage itself, meaning you can still be playing an ego game, only it is now camouflaged as spiritual behavior. For most spiritual people their egos would love to make them think they do not need to study this book or can ignore some of its points. This would be highly unfortunate for those who want to make true spiritual progress.

Where ego games come from

An ego game is a set of outer behaviors and beliefs designed to keep you trapped in a pattern. The purpose of keeping you trapped is to ensure the fulfillment of the ego's goals. As explained in the previous book, the ego is born from duality and duality always has two opposite polarities that seem like contradictions. The ego is full of contradictions. The goals of the ego are also contradictory, which means they can never actually be fulfilled.

Sooner or later the ego will have created such a mess in your outer circumstances and your mind that the Conscious You will be forced to wake up and start taking back charge of your life. The ego will seek to delay this for as long as possible but for most lifestreams it cannot delay it forever. What are some of the goals of the ego? The overall goal is that the ego realizes that it exists but that it is mortal, meaning it has no permanent existence. The ego's primary goal is to ensure its own survival, yet even this has an inescapable contradiction.

The ego knows that it was created by the Conscious You making a decision. The ego knows that if the Conscious You became conscious of the decision that created the ego, the Conscious You could instantly undo that decision and the ego would begin to die. In one sense, the ego knows that in order to survive, it must remain hidden to the Conscious You. From this perspective, it would seem to be best for the ego to keep a low profile and seek to remain small and unnoticed.

The ego is born from duality, and in the duality consciousness anything seems possible. As explained in the previous book, the duality consciousness thinks it has the ability to define reality. The ego can never see that this is a fallacy, and the ego is firmly trapped in the illusion that if it could only do something spectacular enough, it could get God to accept it as worthy and it would be immortalized.

You now see the inescapable dilemma of the ego. On the one hand it must seek to remain unnoticed by the Conscious You that created it. On the other hand, the ego wants to set itself up as being so important in this world that God simply has to acknowledge its value and immortalize it. Obviously, the more the ego seeks to make itself noticeable in the world, the easier it becomes for the Conscious You to see the ego—if the Conscious You is looking and knows what to look for.

We can say that ego games are designed to keep the Conscious You trapped in a certain pattern. You are so focused on individual trees that you never have the awareness to step back and look at the forest—meaning the ego itself. Ego dramas are designed to give the ego such a status in the material world that God will let it into the spiritual world and immortalize it.

Understanding what ego games do for you

In the previous book we explain that the material universe can be compared to an experience machine that is designed to give the Conscious You any experience it wants until it has had enough of it and wants more. With this in mind, an ego game is not simply something the ego has created in order to keep the Conscious You trapped. An ego game can also have the function of giving the Conscious You the experience that it decided it wanted—the experience you can have only as a separate being.

Take my previous example of people who take pride in being good warriors. You cannot have that experience through the Christ consciousness where you see yourself as part of a whole. You can have it only through the consciousness of anti-christ where you can believe in the illusion that you are separated from the whole and can harm others without affecting yourself. You can believe that if you are a warrior and kill other people without being hurt, then your killing has no further consequences for yourself.

An ego game originally had the function of giving you an experience that you wanted. Once you have stepped into the perception filter defined by the game, it colors the way you see life. The ego will now seek to use the game to keep you trapped in that pattern indefinitely. In doing so, the ego might be able to use even a spiritual teaching.

In the East, there are many lifestreams who in the past have risen above the more primitive version of wanting to be a warrior who kills with weapons. They still have a desire to be warriors who fight others, perhaps in non-lethal combat. That is why the East has seen the emergence of several systems that merge spiritual teachings with a form of combat, sometimes non-lethal combat.

Some people have started to rise above the need to experience the lowest aspects of being a warrior, but they have not fully risen above it. Their egos have created different versions of the warrior game where you see yourself as a spiritual warrior. The ego can even create games where people see themselves as warriors who are not fighting other people but fighting non-physical forces. Such games can actually be helpful to a lifestream's spiritual growth, but there will come a point where you will be free only by completely leaving behind the ego game and the experience it facilitates. Those who are open to this book should consider that they are either at that point or close to it.

Take note of how this relates to my previous talk about LIFE decisions. Some ego games define who you are, for example that you are a warrior. Once you step into that perception filter, it seems as if the Conscious You does not need to make LIFE decisions related to its identity. After all, you see yourself as a warrior and the ego will never question the validity of this identity. It seems like you could not be anything else and that there is no reason to question that you do what a warrior does.

Of course, being a warrior means struggling against other warriors, and over many lifetimes you might have had enough of this struggle. Many lifestreams have indeed made the LIFE decision that they no longer see themselves as warriors. Others can become stuck in the pattern, thinking they are forced to be warriors because other people attack them or oppose their ultimate cause. They have to keep fighting until the cause is fulfilled, and this is the essence of the ego dramas.

How can you possibly
unmask your own ego
as long as you are always
looking outside yourself?

5 | SECURITY GAMES

In this discourse I will address an ego game that most religious people, even most spiritual seekers, have not understood. If you can come to see through this game and learn to recognize it in your own life, you can take your spiritual growth to an entirely new level. In order to understand this game, let us begin by looking at my statement to Nicodemus:

> And no man hath ascended up to heaven, but he
> that came down from heaven... (John 3:13)

Traditionally, this has been a mysterious quote that most Christians have found it difficult to interpret. Let me give you a deeper understanding. I have explained that the core of your being is the Conscious You. If this concept is new to you, simply take a moment and become aware that you are sitting "here," reading this discourse. Instead of being absorbed in reading, you are now conscious that you are a "self" reading these words. You have mentally stepped outside your current situation, and you are no longer fully identified with it.

Where does this ability come from? It comes from the fact that you *are* the Conscious You and that this

Conscious You is an extension of God's own Being. This is what gives you self-awareness because the Creator has individualized its universal, omnipresent self-awareness for and as your localized self-awareness. This means you are more than anything in this world, including your body, outer mind and material circumstances.

As a result, the Conscious You has the ability to return to the awareness of who it really is and stop identifying itself with and as any identity you have built during your sojourn in the material realm. This is also what gives you the ability to mentally step outside a particular ego game, see it for what it is and make the decision to separate yourself from the game by no longer identifying yourself with the illusions that propagate the game and turn it into a catch-22.

The Conscious You is the "man" who descended from heaven and it has the ability to ascend back to heaven. In contrast, the sense of identity based on the illusions of duality – what many people call the soul – does *not* have the ability to ascend back to heaven. As explained, the ego was born out of your separation from your own higher being, and the ego has built a mortal sense of identity for you.

Now, at this point I am deliberately facing you with a choice. You may have been programmed by your previous spiritual world view to believe that the soul – or mortal identity – can somehow be saved, that it can become acceptable in the eyes of God and gain entry into heaven. Most religious people believe this and even most spiritual seekers or New Age people believe the same although based on a different reasoning.

I am deliberately challenging you to question this belief and your reasons for accepting it. If you are not willing to question the idea that the mortal identity can somehow be saved or resurrected, then you have no chance of escaping the ego game I am addressing in this discourse. You will indefinitely be condemned to repeating that game, seeking for ever more sophisticated ways to do what is truly impossible, but which the ego will never see as impossible. For those who have ears to hear, let me move on to explaining why the ego's game is truly impossible.

Understanding why death cannot overcome death

Let me briefly summarize the process of Creation [For more about this, see *The Power of Self*]. You were created as an extension of the Creator. You were meant to grow in self-awareness from a very localized sense of self toward the state of mind in which you experience oneness with your source and oneness with all life—what is commonly called "enlightenment."

This process was meant to happen under the guidance of a loving, spiritual teacher and with your awareness that you are part of something greater than your localized self. You would never feel alone or abandoned but instead feel your Creator's unconditional love for you.

The process was also meant to happen as a result of your free-will choices, for that is truly the only way you can grow in self-awareness. Self-awareness can only come from within, it cannot be forced upon you from without. Free will inevitably gave rise to the possibility that you could choose to separate yourself from your teacher and forget about your spiritual source, even come to believe there is no God and no higher reality to your own being.

If you had not chosen separation, you would have grown in Christ consciousness because "Christ" is the term for the universal awareness that is designed to maintain oneness between the Creator and its creation. The separation could happen only as a result of you choosing to experiment with the consciousness of anti-christ, eventually becoming so blinded by it that you lost your awareness of your Self as an immortal spiritual being and came to see yourself as a mortal human being, perhaps even as a sinner by nature.

Before you separated yourself from your teacher, you had a sense of identity as an extension of a greater Being, as being part of the Body of God. The separation literally caused this sense of self to die, and instead a new sense of self was born, a self based on the illusion that you are a separate being who is disconnected from God and from other separate beings. This is a mortal sense of self because it is based on an illusion and created with an inescapable fear of annihilation, a fear of death.

In contrast, the Conscious You cannot die, for it is an extension of the Creator's Being. The Conscious You can create and accept any identity it chooses, and it can believe it is a mortal being, accepting the fear that comes with such a sense of identity. We might say that this causes the Conscious You to go through a form of spiritual death—however it can be resurrected from that state of death, which is what I came to demonstrate.

The essential realization is that the separate self is the ego, or at least the seed of the ego. The ego is born from separation, and the ego has built a sense of identity for you that is based on the illusion of separation, the consciousness of duality. Because the ego was not created by God but is born from unreality, *it can never be saved, it can never enter the kingdom of god*. Which means that the ego can never overcome the fear of annihilation, the fear of death.

When the Conscious You begins to accept – identify with – the mortal identity created by the ego, it is inevitable that you will feel the fear of death. This is a fear that you simply cannot live with in its full intensity. You have to find a way to reduce this fear to a level of intensity that you can live with. You cannot escape the fear until you separate yourself from the ego, but you can push it aside so it is somewhat livable. You now have the foundation for understanding the basic dynamic of the ego:

• Your ego is born from your sense of separation from your own higher being, your I AM Presence.

• Your ego has created a sense of identity that is based on separation.

• Separation is unreal and thus the ego's identity is unreal, meaning it cannot live forever—it is mortal.

• The consequence is that the ego can never escape the fear of death. When the Conscious You accepts the mortal identity as its real self, you too will feel the fear of death.

• You cannot live with the fear of death, and you are compelled to look for a way out.

• The very central dynamic of the ego is that it must constantly seek for ways to neutralize the fear of death so that you can live with it. It must do so in such a way that you do *not* discover the real way out, namely to return to your original identity as an immortal spiritual being. If you do, the ego will die and you will ascend.

• Because the ego has a survival instinct, it will do anything to prevent you from discovering that the ego is based on an illusion but that you are real. It will do anything to prevent you from questioning the mortal identity and the illusions upon which it is based.

• In order to neutralize the fear of death, the ego must create the illusion that the mortal self can be saved, can somehow become immortal and does not have to die. When the Conscious You believes this, you will believe that *you* can be saved without giving up or separating yourself from the mortal self.

• In reality, this is a losing battle, for the Conscious You can never fully forget its intuitive knowledge that there must be more to life—that there is more to *you*.

• The ego is very skillful in postponing your return to your spiritual identity – the process of enlightenment – and it has come up with innumerable subtle schemes for doing so. This is what I called the "broad way that leads to destruction."

You cannot fool God

Once you understand this dynamic, you see something extremely important. You see that the ego's mortal sense of identity is based on the illusions of duality, the illusions of anti-christ. Precisely because the ego cannot see beyond duality, its attempts to make it seem like the mortal self can be saved are also based on duality. The ego is seeking to save the mortal self – created from the consciousness of death – by using the same consciousness that created it. The ego is seeking to solve a problem with the same state of consciousness that created the problem. It is seeking to compensate for one illusion by creating another illusion.

You can then begin to realize that there truly is no way to fool God. Even if your ego can fool you and every other person on this planet, God clearly sees the distinction between the reality of Christ and the unreality of anti-christ. The Conscious You can enter heaven at any time, but this cannot happen while you identify yourself with or as a mortal being. The only way to be saved – attain the eternal life that takes you beyond the fear of death – is to return to your true identity as a spiritual being—and that can only happen when you let the mortal self die. There simply is no other way to salvation than the path of oneness—even though the ego and the false teachers have created a seemingly much easier and better way that they claim will take you to salvation without letting the mortal self die. As I explained:

13 Enter ye in at the strait gate: for wide is the gate, and broad is the way, that leadeth to destruction, and many there be which go in thereat:
14 Because strait is the gate, and narrow is the way, which leadeth unto life, and few there be that find it.
(Matthew, Chapter 7)

The ego is seeking to use the death consciousness to neutralize the fear of death and this can never work. Before we move on, let me mention that the false path offered by the ego and the false teachers offers certain advantages—the main one being that you do not have to take full responsibility for yourself. It was your refusal to take this responsibility that took you onto the false path in the first place. Nevertheless, the seeming advantages of the path are only relative advantages.

For example, the ego can help you live with the fear of death, but it was the ego that gave rise to that fear in the first place. The ego is only offering to help reduce the consequences of the problem it has created—which will never remove the problem but only help the ego stay alive. While this can work for a time, you will eventually begin to feel that the "advantages" offered by the ego are empty and do not satisfy your inner longing for something more to life.

You will see many people who are still satisfied by the ego's mortal identity and the "advantages" it offers. You will also see a growing number of people who have begun to feel dissatisfied with their present identity and long for something more. That longing is the beginning of spiritual progress, but you will make significant progress only when you begin to see that the "advantages" offered by the ego are really disadvantages in that they take away your freedom and lock you in a mental box. As an example, consider fundamentalist religion, which claims its members will be saved but also causes its members to accept a very limited and fear-based outlook on life.

How the ego creates a false sense of security

The ego seeks to compensate for the fear of death by creating a sense of absolute security. It does this by making it seem like the mortal self can be saved or that the fear of death is unnecessary or irrational.

The ego game I am addressing in this discourse is the security game, the game of creating the impression that your entry into the kingdom of God – a realm that is beyond the material universe – can be secured by you living up to certain conditions *in* the material universe. It is an attempt to use the consciousness of separation to secure your entry into the realm of oneness—whereas the only way to be "saved" is to give up the illusion of separation and return to the oneness in which you were created—eventually expanding it to the ultimate oneness.

Precisely because the ego and the false teachers of humankind have been so successful in promoting the false path to salvation, many spiritual and religious people will be reluctant to admit the reality I am stating here. The dividing line is simple. Those who are still too identified with the mortal selves created by their egos will be unwilling to acknowledge reality because it will be too big of a threat to their sense of security. Their sense of equilibrium is based on the belief that because of certain conditions in this world, they are guaranteed to be saved. It would be too big of a shock to admit that their basic world view is a fallacy.

The only people who can acknowledge what I am saying are those who have started to separate themselves from the mortal identity. They have some sense that they are more than the mortal identity and they sense intuitively that they will not die when their mortal selves die. As a result, they can question the belief that the mortal identity can be saved. Some will even be willing to see that it is futile to use the ideas springing from the consciousness of anti-christ to attain entry into the kingdom of God. Only the Christ mind can enter, and the only solution is for you to: "let this mind be in you which was also in Christ Jesus," as Paul put it. Such people can then take a quantum leap forward on the spiritual path by beginning a process of systematically separating themselves from the false path and its many disguises. Let us take a closer look.

Overcoming the illusion of an automatic salvation

Throughout history any number of religions have made the claim that their members would automatically be saved. Even today, you find many religions that claim the same. For example, many fundamentalist Christians believe that I will soon appear in the sky to judge humankind and that all who are good-standing members of their church will automatically be saved simply by being members of this outer, earthly organization—or by declaring me as their Lord and Savior. They conveniently overlook that I said:

20 And when he was demanded of the Pharisees, when
the kingdom of God should come, he answered them
and said, The kingdom of God cometh not with obser-
vation:
21 Neither shall they say, Lo here! or, lo there! for,
behold, the kingdom of God is within you. (Luke, Chapter 17)

The deeper meaning is, of course, that there is no such
thing as an automatic salvation. This belief is the extreme outcome of the ego's desire for ultimate security. For example,
many previous civilizations believed that there was a special
class of people who were fundamentally different from the
masses simply by their birth. This gave rise to the feudal system where it was believed that people from the noble class had
different physical properties, such as blue blood, and also had
special mental abilities and were favored by the gods.

When this is transferred to the field of religion, we see the
belief that members of a particular religion are favored by God,
and this is especially true of the priesthood of that religion.
This mindset was directly responsible for the early Christian
church gradually elevating me to a superior status, culminating
in the Nicene creed that declared me to be the only begotten
Son.

When you study my discourse on black-and-white thinking, [see *Freedom From Ego Illusions*] you will see that the
belief in an automatic salvation is a direct outcome of this sim-
plistic form of thinking. It gives rise to the belief that there
can be only one true religion, and it follows that the members
of that religion must have a special status, meaning they will
automatically be saved.

The ego loves this black-and-white logic because once you
believe in it, it is extremely difficult for you to extricate yourself

from that mental box. The reason is that black-and-white thinking implies that it is dangerous – in an ultimate way, such as burning forever in hell – to think outside the box defined by the only true religion. The ego can then feel secure that you will not question the sense of identity it has created for you, for example as a "good Christian." A sense of identity which the ego claims will one day be saved whereas the reality is that it will keep you outside the kingdom of oneness indefinitely.

Because the ego cannot see reality, it actually believes it can be saved, and it will do anything to keep you in that limited identity. As long as you do not question the ego's basic world view, the ego feels secure, and for most people this translates into them feeling secure. After all, why wouldn't you feel secure when you believe you are among the chosen people who are guaranteed to be saved? The cost of this security is that you can never ask questions, which means the Conscious You can never actually satisfy its longing for the "something more to life" that it knows must exist. The ego has created a gilded cage, but a cage nonetheless.

The ego game of security is actually the ego seeking to make itself feel secure because it believes it has managed to put you into a mental box from which you will never see the fact that the ego is unreal. The Conscious You has a built-in longing for oneness with your source. While this longing can be pushed aside or covered over, it can never be satisfied by the ego. Your ego feeling secure will not make you feel "secure," at least not forever.

But what about a guaranteed salvation?

A more subtle version of the security game is the concept that simply being a member of a particular religion is not enough in itself, but that you also need to live up to certain requirements, which can range from outer behavior to a certain focus on overcoming negative or sinful thoughts and emotions. The central premise is still that if you follow certain rules, you will end up meeting the requirements that will guarantee your salvation or your entry into a higher state of consciousness. This can range from Christians going to church and following outer rules to New Age people doing yoga, meditation or other exercises. It can even encompass students of the ascended masters who think invoking spiritual light is – in itself – enough to raise their consciousness.

The problem with this belief system is that it is based on a mechanical view of the world—as is materialistic science and even mainstream Christianity. The idea is that there are mechanical reasons why you need to be saved, such as you having made karma that needs to be balanced. By following certain mechanical procedures, you will automatically balance your karma and then your salvation is guaranteed. Even the belief that I have paid for humankind's sins is a mechanical view that sees sin as a debt that some sacrifice can pay back whereupon God simply has to accept people covered by the sacrifice.

Such a mechanical view of life and salvation is completely out of touch with the reality of life, as described in Maitreya's book and in my course in Christhood. You are not a mechanical being, you are not a robot, but a co-creator with God. This means you are not here to perform some kind of mechanical task whereupon you can ascend to a remote heaven. You are here to act as a co-creator with God who brings heaven to earth by manifesting the abundant life for all people. This simply cannot be done in a mechanical way, as it is your task to express your individual creativity in full measure.

The real key to salvation is not to find some magical formula but to be the being God created—the "man" who descended from heaven. This is a highly individual and creative effort, and there never can be any guarantee that you will fulfill your goal. On the other hand, there is no mechanical standard for how you should – or should not – fulfill that goal, as the main requirement is that you exercise creativity in a way that raises all life.

Of course, true creativity is a stream flowing from your I AM Presence and directed by the Conscious You according to choices you make. Since the ego can never contact your higher being, your ego can never be truly creative. The ego can never see creativity as the key to salvation and it must forever seek for a mechanical way to ensure your salvation. In so doing, it uses the consciousness of anti-christ, which is also mechanical in nature because it too is separated from the Creator's ever-flowing fount of creative life.

If you look at the religious landscape, you will see innumerable systems that seek to define mechanical requirements for how you can qualify for salvation, enlightenment, ascension or whatever you want to call it. They are all built upon the idea that by living up to requirements in the material world, you can force your way into the spiritual world. The stark truth is that you can enter the spiritual state of consciousness only by returning to the state of consciousness in which you were created. As I said:

> 2 And Jesus called a little child unto him, and set him in the midst of them,
> 3 And said, Verily I say unto you, Except ye be converted, and become as little children, ye shall not enter into the kingdom of heaven.
> 4 Whosoever therefore shall humble himself as this little child, the same is greatest in the kingdom of heaven. (Matthew, Chapter 18)

But you must be able to earn your salvation?

At this point I know some spiritual seekers will say that I am contradicting everything they know about the spiritual path, even what is said on our websites. After all, isn't the point of giving decrees and invocations to transform misqualified energy in order to purify one's consciousness?

The key to understanding this is to pay close attention to my teachings that the ego is born from the duality consciousness and cannot see beyond it. Why have you sinned, made karma or misqualified energy? Because you have become blinded by the duality consciousness!

Some people come to the realization that they have sunk or fallen into a lower state, whether they see this as being sinners, having made karma or having descended to a lower state of consciousness. Their egos and the false teachers will now attempt to make them believe that the key to climbing out of that state is to perform some mechanical techniques in order to compensate for the mechanical reasons that caused the descent, be this actions (sin or karma) or negative thoughts/emotions.

The real problem that stands between you and salvation is not your sin, karma or negative energy. These are truly mechanical conditions, but they were created as a result of you being blinded by the duality consciousness. It is absolutely impossible to compensate for the conditions created through duality by using some kind of mechanical means defined by the duality consciousness. You cannot overcome sin through the same consciousness that created the sin, you cannot balance the karma through the same consciousness that generated the karma.

Surely, you can use certain spiritual techniques to balance karma in an almost mechanical way, but unless you change the consciousness that led you to make the karma, you will inevitably make more karma. Your use of such techniques will not produce steady progress, but a see-saw motion of making karma, balancing, karma, making karma and so on until you decide you are willing to look for the beam in your own eye and change your consciousness.

By transforming negative energy you can indeed make it easier for yourself to see through the illusions of duality. This can form the basis for you changing your consciousness, but in order to produce that change, you must make the LIFE decisions I spoke about earlier. Such decisions are creative, not mechanical decisions. You must consciously choose to undo the dualistic beliefs you have accepted.

Accepting a dualistic belief can be done as the result of an unconscious – and mechanical – decision, what I call a death decision. You cannot undo such a decision except by becoming more awake and making a creative decision. That is why there is no mechanical path to salvation, regardless of what the ego and the innumerable ego-based teachers and religious leaders will tell you.

See the pattern in history

If you take an honest look at history, you will see how the ego's impossible quest for security has influenced human behavior and thought systems. It should be obvious how this has worked and is still working in religion, especially fundamentalist religion that is so clearly based on black-and-white thinking. However, this is not limited to the field of religion.

For example, Marxism and Communism is also a dualistic thought system that reduces the complexity of human life to a simple struggle between two classes, defining one as bad and one as good. It proposes a very simple solution in which the state becomes the replacement for the theistic God found in fundamentalist religion. Essentially, the state becomes the source of the automatic salvation so even though Marxism is an atheist belief system, it still allows at least some people to reduce their fear of death to a manageable level.

What I call gray thinking can also be used to reduce the fear of death, often by defining the fear as irrational or defining the problem out of existence. For example, materialistic science attempts to define fear as an irrational emotion that should be suppressed, and this works for some people. Materialism also seeks to define the need for salvation out of existence by denying the spiritual side of life, which allows some people to suppress the fear of not being saved, reducing the fear of death.

Neither a black-and-white nor a gray thought system can ever remove the fear of death. This can be done only by rising above dualistic thinking and truly experiencing that you are an immortal spiritual being who has no need to fear the death of a physical body that you wear as an overcoat and can replace when it is worn out. Of course, your identification with a dualistic identity will prevent you from having such an experience, and that is why the ego and the false teachers have been so successful in creating a catch-22 from which most people have not been able to extricate themselves.

Times are changing rapidly, and it is becoming easier for people to see through the inconsistencies that will – by the fact that they are based on dualistic thinking that always incorporates two opposite polarities – be built into all of the thought systems created by the ego. As the collective consciousness is raised toward the Christic level, people will gradually shed the snake skins of duality, allowing them to become truly free of the fear of death by being reborn into a new self-awareness. As they stop denying their true identity as co-creators with God, people will begin to create a society that is based on the reality of Christ rather than the graven images of anti-christ. This is a society that gives room for creativity rather than seeking to kill it based on a warped attempt to overcome the fear of death through mechanical – anti-creative – means.

This new society will not be dominated by the fear of death, and it will not be controlled by thought systems that aim to compensate for the fear of death by herding people into mental boxes created by the death consciousness. More and more people will leave their nets – the nets that keep them trapped in duality – and let the dead bury their dead. They will stop blindly following the blind leaders but will instead follow the vision they see in their hearts, the vision that is beyond any images created by the ego. People will understand what I said 2,000 years ago:

> I am come that they might have life, and that they might have it more abundantly. (John 10:10)

Seeing the big picture

What keeps you from the abundant life is the ego and its attempts to compensate for separation by creating graven images based on the very consciousness that led to separation. You cannot live like a little child, but you think you have to struggle to get what the material universe is designed to give you without effort:

> Fear not, little flock; for it is your Father's good plea-sure to give you the kingdom. (Luke 12:32)

To get that abundant life, you only need to stop using the dualistic mind to reject it. You need to reach for the non-dualistic truth of Christ:

> If ye continue in my word, then are ye my disciples indeed;
>
> And ye shall know the truth, and the truth shall make you free. (John 8:32-33)

However, in order to be truly free, you cannot hold on to the old, mortal, dualistic identity. You have to be willing to let it die so you can be reborn of water and of Spirit:

> For whosoever will save his life shall lose it: and whosoever will lose his life for my sake shall find it. (Matthew 16:25)
>
> 5 Verily, verily, I say unto thee, Except a man be born of water and of the Spirit, he cannot enter into the kingdom of God.
> 6 That which is born of the flesh is flesh; and that which is born of the Spirit is spirit.
> 7 Marvel not that I said unto thee, Ye must be born again.
> 8 The wind bloweth where it listeth, and thou hearest the sound thereof, but canst not tell whence it cometh, and whither it goeth: so is every one that is born of the Spirit. (John 3:5-8)

That which is born of the flesh seeks a mechanical way to salvation whereas that which is born of the Spirit is willing to be creative.

My real hope for this discourse is to help the more mature students see the big picture. When you look at human beings, you will see a clear tendency that when people have accepted a certain thought system, they will go to great length to defend it. They will even invent reasons for why it must be true and display great intensity in discrediting people or ideas that seem to threaten their "infallible" system. I am hoping to help people acknowledge that whenever you see this response, you will know that behind it is the ego's futile quest for absolute security.

I am hoping that people will begin to see this mechanism in themselves. If you can admit that when you hold on to or defend ideas, it is the ego's quest for security, you can make great progress toward the only true form of security, which is the direct experience of the reality of God that is possible only through the Christ mind.

The ego's quest for ultimate security is not actually wrong—it is simply misguided. In reality, the ego has perverted the very quest that is built into your lifestream, namely the drive to return to oneness with your Creator by raising your self-awareness beyond localization.

I am not asking you to suppress your longing for something ultimate. I am asking you to realize that this longing can never be satisfied by anything in the material world, but only through oneness with your ultimate source. Even if your ego managed to produce a state of ultimate security on earth, the real you would not be satisfied by it.

When you realize this, you can stop defending any of the mental boxes based on duality—and you can begin to free yourself – your sense of self – from being imprisoned in such boxes. You can then understand and live the true meaning of my words:

23 But the hour cometh, and now is, when the true wor-
shippers shall worship the Father in spirit and in truth:
for the Father seeketh such to worship him.
24 God is a Spirit: and they that worship him must worship him in spirit and in truth. (John, Chapter 4)

However, in today's world, I would add that the only way
to truly worship God is to become one with God. That oneness is the ultimate security. The ego will never fathom or
attain it, but the Conscious You *can*.

Am I hereby saying that you should not be attached to any
thought system on earth? That is exactly what I am saying! The
ego can turn any system – no matter how much truth it contains – into a prison for your Being. Simply give up the dream
that there is an ultimate thought system on earth and instead
flow with the River of Life in which you are one with the Spirit
of Truth, the Spirit that can never be confined to any mental
box on earth.

See through the ego's dream of ultimate security based on
separation. Let that dream die so that you can be reborn into
the ultimate security of oneness. I know this is not easy, for the
false belief systems have immense power in the collective consciousness. In order to help people truly overcome the mindset
behind the quest for ego-based security, I will expose the ego's
dramas in the next book in this series.

6 | SURVIVAL GAMES

The story of Doctor Frankenstein was inspired by the ascended masters in order to illustrate one of the fundamental properties of the ego. The plot is simple, namely that a doctor – with seemingly benign motives – stitches together dead body parts and infuses them with life. Once the creature has received a form of life, it displays a survival instinct that makes it willing to kill anyone standing in its way, even its own creator. Because the doctor is unwilling to deal with his creation, he eventually perishes—as does the creature.

This is the basic characteristic of your ego. You took "dead" ideas, meaning ideas and beliefs that sprang from the consciousness of anti-christ, and put them together into a whole. You then used your creative abilities to infuse them with a form of life so that your "creature" could fulfill the role of making most decisions for you, seemingly setting the Conscious You free from the responsibility of making decisions.

What you thought was created to serve you, took on a life of its own, and now it wants to control every aspect of your life. Furthermore, it has a ferocious survival instinct and will do anything to stay alive—even if you decide that you no longer want it. In its most primitive form, the ego is willing to do anything to stay alive, even to the point of killing people that oppose it. The ego is even willing to kill you, and it is unable to see that this will lead to its own destruction. To the ego, the ultimate cause is its own survival, and no price is too high to pay in order to ensure its survival.

The ego will literally do anything that it believes is necessary in order to ensure its own survival. When you compare this to my previous teaching that the ego is born out or your separation from God, you can see the dangerous cocktail. Everything is created from God's being—without him was not anything made that was made. The connecting link between all self-aware beings is God. When you know that you are part of God's being, you also know that other people are part of God's being, and you know, in a very fundamental way, that if you hurt others, you also hurt yourself. As I said:

> And the King shall answer and say unto them, Verily I say unto you, Inasmuch as ye have done it unto one of the least of these my brethren, ye have done it unto me. (Matthew 25:40)

It is truly only when you acknowledge that you have some connection to God that you can follow my commandment to do unto others what you want them to do to you. That is why people who identify with their egos are unwilling to follow this command and even look at is as a primitive or weak statement.

Because the ego is born from your separation from God, it inevitably sees itself as completely separate from other people. The ego believes it can hurt others without harming itself, and this is what gives rise to the most primitive of all ego games, namely that of ultimate physical survival.

Physical survival leading to spiritual death

The Conscious You is able to identify itself as anything it chooses. The same is true for the ego. I have compared the ego to a forest, and the kind of trees you put into the forest will determine the ego's behavior. When a person sinks to the absolute lowest level of human awareness, the ego of that person identifies itself with and as the physical body. The survival and preservation of the physical body becomes the most important goal for the ego. The person will do anything to attain that goal, including killing anyone who is perceived as a threat to the survival of the body.

In previous discourses, I compared the ego to the operating system of a computer. What actually happens when people come to identify with their physical bodies is that the computer program of the ego merges with the computer program that is built into the physical body. The human body/brain is – as most modern people realize – a very complex mechanism.

Many scientists believe all aspects of human consciousness is the result of the physical processes in the brain and nervous system. While this is incorrect, it is to some degree understandable that scientists can reach this conclusion. The brain and nervous system are truly so complex that they give rise to many thoughts and feelings. For people who have forgotten their spiritual identity and have come to identify themselves with and as a physical body, virtually all of their thoughts and feelings are produced by the brain and nervous system receiving and to some degree modifying impulses from the mass consciousness. When the ego merges with the "body computer," the computer programs built into the physical body come to dominate the computer of the ego.

It should not be difficult to see that the programs of the physical body are entirely centered around the survival of the body. This is not to say that this is necessarily wrong or evil. I am not agreeing with the traditional view of many religious people – including many Christians – that the body is evil. A lion is not evil, it simply does what it needs to do in order to survive. Likewise, the body will do what it needs to do in order to survive. The problem is, of course, that the body computer is not actually able to think.

It has only physical life, but no spiritual life. It has no self-awareness and consequently no way to distinguish between what brings it closer to oneness or further into separation. It has no ethical or moral concerns, and it is incapable of reasoning that what it thinks is necessary for its survival might be "wrong" or have long-term consequences for the entity that inhabits the body, namely you. The result is the creation of an ego-game that is programmed to do anything to ensure the short-term and long-term survival of the physical body.

Throughout history, this ego game has taken on many different forms. As an example, consider that during medieval times, most men traveled with a sword. The slightest provocation would be seen as a threat to the person's honor, and the result would be a duel to the death. Numerous people were killed over something that was not an actual physical threat but only a perceived threat. It became a physical threat because of the tradition of settling disputes with a duel. Other obvious examples are how people will kill others in order to steal food or other property. This often leads those who have something worth stealing to build a pattern of automatically killing those who are seen as real or potential threats to their property.

Taking this to a greater scale, we see war as an example of how some soldiers will become perfect killing machines. They automatically kill any enemy solider without even considering any moral or ethical implications. We see a similar tendency in organized crime, even the popular movie image of the crime boss who will kill anyone who threatens the survival of his empire—which he identifies as an extension of his body.

On an even greater scale, entire nations or civilizations can create their version of the survival game. They build the image that other nations are a threat, and they are willing to use whatever weapons or methods are available in order to secure victory. This can be extended to building the image that a particular race or ethnic group is a threat to the survival of another group or nation. Hitler's genocide against the Jews is an obvious example of the ultimate survival game taken to the extreme. The Allied bombing campaign against civilian targets in German cities shows that no nation is immune to this game, as do the atomic bombs dropped over civilian populations in Japan.

Another aspect of this game is that the long-term survival of the physical body requires propagation, and when the ego takes this to the extreme, you get rape. On an even larger scale, you get the many forms of suppression of women, fueled by the male ego's perceived need for the long-term survival of the physical body. This makes it necessary that women are available to fill what the male ego perceives as their main role, namely to be available for propagation.

Rising above physical survival

Obviously, I could continue indefinitely to give examples of how this particular ego game has led to incredible atrocities. This game is behind many of the atrocities seen in history, with the perpetrators often feeling that they had to destroy the "enemy" in order to ensure their own survival. It is the old adage: "It was him or me!"

I trust most spiritual seekers clearly see the primitive nature of this game. The reason why you can see this is that most spiritual seekers – and certainly most of the people open to this book – have risen above the most primitive ego-game. I start out describing the more primitive games specifically to help you see that you have already risen above some of the ego's games. Surely, you would not indiscriminately kill anyone you perceived as a threat, and hopefully you would not kill anyone no matter what the situation. This is a clear sign that you have already started separating the Conscious You from complete identification with the ego. It is by continuing this process that you will eventually win the victory of attaining the Christ consciousness.

In order to complete the process, you need to consciously understand how you can separate yourself from the ego. Doing this unconsciously is a good first step, but becoming a mature spiritual student requires that you come to a conscious awareness and understanding of the spiritual path and what it entails. You can only climb so high on the path without conscious awareness. To reach the higher levels, you must begin to see exactly how the ego seeks to hide behind the trees in the forest.

How can a person begin the process of overcoming the most primitive ego game and rise from functioning as a mere animal to becoming a spiritual being in a physical body? The core of the process is that the Conscious You of the person must begin to realize that it is more than the body and then more than the ego. However, when a person is fully identified with the ego and when that person's ego is fully identified with the physical body, there is little possibility of reaching that person with a spiritual message of any kind. Many people literally will be awakened only by having their physical bodies killed over and over again, until it begins to dawn on the Conscious You that it is not the body. This happens because a violent death will burn a scar in the person's soul that will carry over as (often partially subconscious) memories in succeeding lives, giving the person a memory that it can survive the death of the body.

As explained, the material universe acts as a kind of mirror that reflects back physical circumstances that correspond to your state of consciousness. When you identify yourself with and as the body – and become trapped in the game of ensuring the survival of the body – you will enter a state of consciousness where you are constantly looking for threats to the body. The subconscious message you are sending out is that you live in a world where everything is a potential threat, and the universe obediently reflects back to you physical circumstances in which you encounter such threats. For example, many people involved with gangs or organized crime have precipitated a situation where they are under constant threat—and all of the people involved are simply playing their roles in the collective drama they have created through their individual minds. They have gravitated together because of their similar states of mind, and now they are threatening each other in order to outplay their internal conflicts.

The ultimate survival game will cause people to precipitate physical circumstances in which they are likely to have their bodies killed. When you seek to save your life, you will lose it, as I said 2,000 years ago. This is actually a safety mechanism whereby the universe outplays people's states of mind so they can receive opportunities for overcoming them. When a person has been killed enough times, the Conscious You of that person will – in between embodiments – begin to realize one of two things:

- It is more than the body.

- It has had enough of the ultimate survival game of always fighting other people.

The person comes into its next embodiment with a sense that it is more than the body or that it no longer wants to fight other people. This is the beginning of an upward spiral. As the Conscious You of the person – often over many embodiments – disassociates itself more and more from the body and the material world, the person will come into embodiment with a conscious awareness that it has a longing for something beyond this world. This can then cause the person to find a spiritual teaching and begin a conscious path toward greater understanding.

Obviously, as a spiritual teacher, I would love to see people awaken from the ultimate survival game without having to be killed numerous times, but unfortunately that is not a likely scenario. Most people who get trapped in this game can only grow out of it when the School of Hard Knocks has given them so many knocks that they begin to think there must be a better way. Some people literally have to be hit on one cheek many times before they begin to realize that until you start turning the other cheek, the blows will keep coming. The reason being that the universe is simply mirroring back what you are sending out so you are creating the blows—even though other people execute them.

Breaking the survival game

As I said, the ego is simply a computer, and it will mindlessly continue to fight the external enemy, never realizing that it is the consciousness of thinking there is an enemy that creates or precipitates the enemy. It is only the Conscious You of a person who has the awareness to be able to think and reason that if it starts turning the other cheek, then the universe will eventually stop sending the enemy. For this to happen, the Conscious You must awaken and decide to take back its responsibility for making decisions. Of course, it was the Conscious You's denial of this responsibility that created the ego and then created the slide toward the ultimate survival game.

Before a person can fully leave the ultimate survival game behind, the person's Conscious You must be willing to acknowledge that it creates its own reality. It must come to understand that the universe truly is a mirror, and the physical conditions it faces will never change until it changes its consciousness. In order to begin this process, the Conscious You must – consciously – override the programming of the ego. The ego will blindly fight the external enemy, and in a sense having such an enemy can become the ultimate excuse for not taking responsibility for your life.

When the Conscious You identifies itself with the ego, it will reason that as long as there is an external enemy, it has to focus all of its awareness on fighting the enemy so there is no time or attention for taking responsibility for changing your consciousness. A soldier who is in the midst of a battle is not very open to working on his psychological issues. Surviving by destroying the enemy takes precedence over anything else.

I trust people open to this book can see how this becomes a catch-22. You create the outer enemy through your state of consciousness. Once the outer enemy is there, the existence of the enemy becomes an excuse for not taking a look at your state of consciousness. It is the perfect excuse for focusing on the splinter in the eye of another and refusing to look at the beam in your own eye. Obviously, the outer enemy will not go away until you change your state of consciousness so that you can turn the other cheek to the blows coming from the enemy. This is the deeper understanding behind my command to turn the other cheek. I am fully aware that most people could not understand that command 2,000 years ago and most still do not understand it. But many are ready to understand that because they have – for many lifetimes – been in a state of consciousness of fighting outer enemies – there is only one way to break that pattern. They *must* stop fighting the outer enemies and allow themselves to be hit on one cheek—and then deliberately turn the other cheek without striking back.

Only by doing this can they send a new message into the cosmic mirror, the message that they no longer want to fight an external enemy. When this has been done enough times – and you might remember that I told my disciples to forgive seventy times seven – the old pattern – created over many lifetimes – will be broken and the universe will now reflect back physical circumstances that correspond to your new state of consciousness. Even though many people are still trapped in the ultimate survival game, you will no longer encounter them and will be able to live at a higher level even though you are still on this planet.

More subtle versions of the survival game

As explained, there are four levels of this world, corresponding to four levels of your mind. The lowest level is the physical level, corresponding to part of your subconscious and conscious minds. The next level up is the emotional, which obviously corresponds to your feelings. After that comes the mental level, which corresponds to your thoughts, but specifically higher thoughts of reason and logic. Finally, we have the etheric or identity level, which corresponds to your sense of identity, meaning how you see yourself, God and the world.

So far, I have talked about the survival game as a purely physical phenomenon, relating to the survival of the body and causing people to be willing to physically kill others in order to ensure their own survival. The survival game also has a version on each of the higher levels, and we will look at each version. As we go up from the physical level, we go toward deeper layers, toward the underlying causes of the survival game. We can then begin to see that even the physical game is not entirely physical. In many cases, people will kill only when they are influenced by very strong emotions, such as fear or anger. Such emotions spring from certain beliefs that again come from the person's sense of identity.

The next step up from the physical level is the emotional, and there is a blurred line between people who are caught in the physical survival game and those who are in the emotional survival game. Obviously, if you are at war and an enemy soldier comes at you with a gun, your life is physically threatened. Many of the people who are trapped in the survival game will kill others when they are not actually threatened but feel that they are threatened. Some will indiscriminately kill those who make them angry or trigger their fear of death.

Most of the civilized world has risen to a level of consciousness where physically killing someone is seen as unacceptable behavior. There are many people who have risen above the physical survival game in the sense that they will not automatically kill those who seem to threaten them. Many of these people have simply put a restriction on their physical behavior without actually resolving the psychological issues that drive that behavior. They are still driven by violent and unresolved emotions. If they become really afraid or really angry, they can no longer restrain their physical behavior and they will kill someone in a fit of passion. There are also many people who have come to the point where even intense rage or fear will not trigger the response of physically killing someone. Nevertheless, these people are still willing to kill someone emotionally.

Killing with psychic energy

It is of continuous amazement to the ascended masters that modern civilization knows the scientific fact that everything is energy, yet people have not been willing to acknowledge the philosophical consequences of this. If your emotional and mental state can have – as has been proven over an over again – an effect on your physical health – either making you sick or preventing you from recovering – then it follows that other people's thoughts and feelings can have an effect on you—and vice versa.

Your body is surrounded by an energy field that is connected to your mind. This energy field can potentially be invaded by the energy impulses produced by other people's thoughts and feelings. It is possible to commit psychic murder by producing such intense waves of psychic energy that it can cause another person to become ill or experience an accident. There are people who are so trapped in the emotional version of the survival game that they will – usually without being consciously aware of it – actually seek to kill someone emotionally by sending intense anger at them.

There are also those who seek to control others through their emotions, and this game is an extension of the survival game. You seek to control others in order to prevent them from becoming a threat. For example, many people seek to control those closest to them through guilt by making others feel obligated to take care of their needs. Some have managed to permanently manipulate their supposed "loved ones" into never going beyond certain boundaries—because if they did, the person in control would feel threatened. There are innumerable specific versions of such control games, and we will take a closer look later. There is also a version of the emotional survival game that has the aim of stirring up other people's emotions so that the manipulator can steal their spiritual energy. When a person sinks into the deeper layers of the duality consciousness, that person can no longer receive spiritual light directly from his or her I AM Presence. This light is necessary for a person's survival so now the person has to steal energy, or light, from a person who is still receiving it from above. This can be done by manipulating other people's emotions, for example by making them angry.

When you misqualify energy in anger, other people can literally steal your light and use it to survive at their – lower – level of consciousness. There are people who are so adept at this emotional survival game that they are literally energy vampires who routinely milk certain people by stirring up their emotions. As an example, consider how someone will seek to draw you into an argument that continues until the person suddenly seems to have had enough, and the argument is over. The reason being that the person has had his or her fill of energy and will now leave you alone until the next "feeding time."

In short, if you recognize that you are regularly taken over by very strong emotions – especially anger and fear that stem from feeling threatened by others – you should recognize that you have not yet risen above the emotional version of the survival game. Another thing to watch out for is that you find it difficult to deal with a situation where other people display strong emotions. There are people who think they have their emotions under control, but they have simply learned to suppress them. In certain situations, their emotions will be stirred, and this is a sign that you are not at peace. You then need to use tools to get greater clarity, including the many forms of therapy available today, and use decrees and invocations to resolve the energies and beliefs that cause you to be trapped in the game of emotional survival.

The mental survival game

At the mental level, we are dealing with ideas and beliefs, for example your religious beliefs. History is filled with examples of how people can be willing to physically kill others because of an idea. If you think that your religion is the only true one and that the devil is opposing it through other people, you might be willing to kill those people, even though they obviously do not threaten you physically. The same, of course, can be the case for people with strong political beliefs, such as the leaders of certain communist and fascist countries.

Behind the willingness to kill over an idea is the belief that the end can justify the means. This belief has been used to justify any number of atrocities, including many subtle versions where people have felt they were fighting for a just cause and that this justified killing others. You can find any number of examples where people have justified the killing of others by thinking that the survival of their idea was more important than the lives of other people. Even democracy was born in bloodshed.

Behind this is the illusion that killing others was the only way to make their idea survive. Look at the example I attempted to set with my mission. I told people to not resist evil and to turn the other cheek. I demonstrated that I was not willing to kill others but I was willing to let them kill me—which actually ensured the survival of the idea I came to promote.

I am fully aware that many Christians have felt that ensuring the survival of their version of Christianity justified the killing of others. But can you seriously believe that – given the teachings and example just described – I am in approval of such behavior? The simple fact is that the idea that the end can justify the means springs from the consciousness of anti-christ. This state of mind is based on separation, which makes it possible to separate the end and the means, saying that in order to accomplish a greater good it is justified to use means that would otherwise be seen as wrong. In the Christ mind no such separation is possible, and it is never acceptable to use means that are in violation of God's law, such as the command that thou shalt not kill. In the Christ mind you can see peaceful ways to promote your idea, ways that are simply obscured for people trapped in the duality of anti-christ. Such people think the only way to ensure the survival of their idea is to use violence.

Again, modern civilization makes it unacceptable for many people to physically kill those who oppose your beliefs. Many people have restrained the actual physical attempts to kill others over ideas. As is the case with emotions, your thoughts are also energy impulses that can be sent like arrows into the minds – energy fields – of other people. There are many people who are engaged in a mental survival game that makes them feel threatened by anyone who opposes or ignores the beliefs that they consider the absolute and infallible truth.

There are many people who see themselves as being good, loving and peaceful people because they think they would never physically kill someone else. This might actually be true, but many of these people are simply unwilling to admit that they are engaged in a battle to kill the beliefs of others. Some aggressively seek to convince others that their beliefs are wrong, and some are even willing to destroy another person's belief in order to defend their own beliefs. For example, you see many scientifically minded people who are deliberately and aggressively trying to destroy other people's belief in religion—any religion. You also see religious people who are trying to destroy the beliefs of people from other religions.

Such "mental warfare" may take the form of verbal arguments, yet for people trapped in the survival game, there is often an underlying aggressive intent. These people are – sometimes knowingly and sometimes without being aware of it – sending certain thoughts into the subconscious minds of others for the purpose of weakening their minds. This form of aggressive mental suggestion can often confuse people so they cannot concentrate or clarify their thoughts and are not effective in a debate (many politicians and media people are very adept at this form of black magic). There is also a mental version of the attempt to steal energy from other people. This is done by forcing them to doubt their beliefs, which then makes them engage in feelings such as fear or anger, causing them to misqualify energy that other people can steal.

I am not here saying that there is anything wrong with taking a stand for what you believe in, yet there is a very subtle distinction that must be made. God has given all people free will so another person has a right to believe whatever he or she wants. You have a right to believe what you want, and you have a right to seek to convince another person of your beliefs. If you do this from the underlying sense of either being threatened or feeling superior, it is inevitable that you will engage in a subtle or overt attempt to force the other person into accepting your beliefs. This aggressive mental suggestion is a clear violation of the Law of Free Will—meaning that you will make karma for doing so, no matter how benign you think your intentions are.

The real distinction here is whether you are seeking to convince others out of a personal need to protect your own – fragile – beliefs that you feel are threatened (only beliefs that are fragile can be threatened), or whether you are coming from a genuine desire to help other people make the best possible choices? Are you seeking to enlighten others so they can make better choices – setting them free to make whatever choices they want – or are you seeking to force them into agreeing with you because this fills your need for security, meaning survival? How do you know whether you are trapped in the mental survival game? Ask yourself these questions:

•   Do you feel threatened when other people question or disagree with your beliefs or your belief system? Upward of 90 percent of the spiritual and religious people on this planet feel this way about their spiritual/religious belief system.

•   Do you constantly find yourself in situations where you have to defend your beliefs or where you are attacking the beliefs of others? Are you engaged in – perhaps consumed by – a dualistic struggle against other people's beliefs?

•   Do you feel you are on a mission to convert others and that your efforts have epic importance in the cosmic battle between good and evil?

•   Do you feel that your belief system is the only true one or the superior one and that other people will not be saved unless they accept your belief system?

•   Do you become very insistent, perhaps even aggressive, in defending your belief system?

•   Do you lapse into strong negative emotions when you feel your belief system is threatened? All negative emotions spring from fear. Anger is simply a disguised attempt to destroy the threat that causes the fear.

• How far are you willing to go in order to refute the arguments of other people? Are you willing to destroy their beliefs in the process?

• Do you feel other people would be better off if they let you tell them what to believe?

• Do you fear that some revelation could undermine or threaten your beliefs?

• Can you identify a tendency to push aside or explain away any questions or doubts concerning your belief system? Do you perhaps react with indifference, meaning that you have numbed yourself as a non-aggressive way to ensure the survival of your beliefs—if you don't feel anything, you can't feel threatened.

• Is your spiritual and religious world view based on something outer, something in this world, such as a specific religion, doctrine or even a guru? Do you fear that if serious doubt was raised about your religion, scripture or guru, your spiritual world view could collapse?

• Does your belief system give you a sense of security—a feeling that you are saved by belonging to this belief system? Can you begin to see that as long as your sense of security is based on a belief system in this world, it can – and will – be threatened? The reason being that it is a house built on sand.

The only way to rise above the sense that your beliefs are threatened is to go within and establish a direct connection to your I AM Presence. You can be truly at peace only when you have replaced outer beliefs with inner knowing of who you really are—for your thoughts are only the products of your sense of identity.

The factor that determines whether you are on the strait and narrow path that leads to eternal life or whether you are on the broad way that leads to destruction is how you identify yourself. In a sense, the physical, emotional and mental survival games are simply attempts to defend your ego-based sense of identity. Do you accept the sense of identity that the ego has built for you or do you accept the identity with which you were created? Is your identity based on the things of this world or is it beyond this world?

The identity survival game

As revealed to Moses, the name of God is "I AM." The ultimate way to take the Lord's name in vain is to attach a concept to the word "I AM" that limits your identity to anything in this world. Consider how people use the words "I am." I am a man, I am a woman, I am a Jew, I am a Black person, I am a Christian, I am a Buddhist, I am an American, I am a Frenchman, I am a doctor, I am a farmer, I am this, I am that. All of these "I am" statements reveal that the vast majority of the people on this planet have built a sense of identity that is defined by the outer divisions and characteristics of this world. All of these worldly identities are mortal, and they must die before you can enter the kingdom of God. This is what I expressed as clearly as I could in this statement:

For whosoever will save his life shall lose it: and whosoever will lose his life for my sake shall find it. (Matthew
16:25)

The life that you shall lose is the sense of identity that is
based on this world. Only by losing this sense of life, only by
letting your worldly sense of identity die, will you find the eternal life of the Christ consciousness—where you identify yourself as a spiritual being, as a son or daughter of God. Because
Christianity became a sectarian religion – rather than the universal spiritual movement I intended – the word "Christ" has
a sectarian ring. It was originally a universal term, intended to
indicate something that is entirely beyond this world.

Many people call themselves Christians, and they think
they are the only ones who will be allowed to enter heaven.
The stark reality is that there are no Christians in heaven—at
least not according to the definition of "Christian" used on
earth. In heaven there are only beings who have permanently
risen above the consciousness of duality, the consciousness
of anti-christ. How can you do this? You can do so only by
leaving all earthly, dualistic identities behind—by letting them
die. If you identify yourself as a Christian – defined in opposition to non-Christians – that dualistic identity will prevent you
from entering heaven.

Who are you then? You are a co-creator with your God,
and you are here to have dominion over the earth—rather than
allowing the earth to have dominion over you by causing you
to define your identity based on worldly divisions. There are
no Christians in Heaven, for in heaven you find only Christed
beings. There are no Christians in heaven—only Christs.

A Christed being has risen above all worldly sense of
identity, for any worldly sense of identity will create a chasm
between your Conscious You and your I AM Presence. This

chasm will prevent you from developing the correct, Christ-like identity that I described when I exclaimed: "I and my father are one" (John 10:30). As a Christed being, you no longer identify yourself based on any characteristics on earth. You identify yourself as an individualization of, as an extension of, your Creator and you know you are here to bring the life and the truth of God into this world—you are here to be the light of the world.

Take note of the subtle distinction here—a distinction that cannot be grasped by the ego. The ego seeks to maintain a separate sense of identity according to which you are an independent being that is separated from God and can do whatever you want. You are a law unto yourself instead of being an expression of God's law. It is this separate, dualistic identity that needs to die before you can reclaim your true identity as a co-creator with God.

The ego will never be able to let this identity die, and it will forever seek to come up with ultimate and infallible arguments for why you should not let that identity die. It will seek to make you believe that if your worldly identity dies, *you* will die. As long as you believe in these arguments, you are trapped in the ultimate survival game—the survival of the separate, dualistic sense of identity that is based on the illusions and the lies of anti-christ. You are – literally – one of the living dead, those who are dead in a spiritual sense because they do not have the true, spiritual life of Christ in them. You are seeking to ensure the survival of an identity that is entirely based on an illusion and can never survive in the long run.

You are engaged in the impossible quest of seeking to make the mortal identity immortal and you believe the ego—who sees the Living Christ as the enemy who has come to destroy it. Truly, the Living Christ *has* come to destroy the ego so that you can become free from the illusion that you are a mortal identity defined by this world. The Christ is come to help you reclaim your true identity as an immortal spiritual being. That is why those who seek to save their – mortal – lives will lose those lives whereas those who are willing to let their mortal selves die in order to be reborn into a new spiritual identity will find eternal life in their new Christlike identity. We can also say that seeking to defend your mortal identity is an all-consuming task that literally eats up your life and prevents you from having the abundant life on earth. By defending the ego's sense of life, you lose both the abundant life on earth and the eternal life beyond earth.

Can you see the irony that the harder you hold on to life, the more sure you are of losing it? The only way to truly hold on to life is to let go of everything in this world. I told people this 2,000 years ago, but very few have understood my message:

> 59 And he said unto another, Follow me. But he said, Lord, suffer me first to go and bury my father.
> 60 Jesus said unto him, Let the dead bury their dead: but go thou and preach the kingdom of God.
> 61 And another also said, Lord, I will follow thee; but let me first go bid them farewell, which are at home at my house.
> 62 And Jesus said unto him, No man, having put his hand to the plow, and looking back, is fit for the kingdom of God. (Luke, Chapter 9)

It is time for me to have a return harvest from my sowing on earth. Will you be one of those who are willing to give up the mortal life in order to follow me into the abundant life?

7 | POWER AND WINNING GAMES

As I have described, the ego's dilemma is that while it wants to remain unseen by the Conscious You, it wants to be seen by the world and by its self-created god. In its attempt to build status with its god, the ego must seek to build status in the world. The ego does not see that it can never achieve status with the real God and it believes that its self-created god will respect its self-defined criteria for what it means to have status on earth. Of course, when several people are all trying to build status by being more important than others, there will inevitably be a power play between them.

The survival games can be somewhat passive in nature in the sense that if the ego does not feel threatened, people can be non-aggressive. You do see examples of local communities, even nations, where people have become so homogenous that the egos of individuals feel quite secure. People can get along peacefully by playing the same ego games yet there is not much real spiritual growth in such a community. Everyone simply lives within the perception filters of their egos.

You even see that different groups or nations can attain a state peace and cooperation where they have come to an unspoken agreement. If one group does not threaten the egos of another group and vice versa, then both can feel secure and there is no need for a power play between them. Obviously, this is not the real peace that passes understanding, but a relative peace built on the logic of the ego. It will not last because, as I have explained, the universe will inevitably precipitate circumstances that in the ego's distorted perception will seem like a threat.

When it comes to the desire to be seen in the world and by its own god, then obviously these power games are not in any way passive in nature. As I said, the ego thinks it can attain status in the eyes of its god by attaining power on earth. Because of the dualistic logic, the ego will literally believe that if it attains some ultimate status or power on earth, then it will be able to force or buy its way into heaven. The ego actually believes that God and the representatives of the Cosmic Christ mind can be forced or persuaded by earthly power. It thinks that if enough people on earth recognize its status, then God must do the same.

Given this belief – and the fact that the ego will never see its fallacy – it is obvious that once people have decided that they want ultimate power on earth, there is no limit to how far they will go and what means they will use in order to attain that power—and in order to secure it once attained. It is also obvious that there will at any given time be more than one person or group of people seeking ultimate power. If two or more people seek ultimate power, then there will inevitably be a struggle between them, for only one can have ultimate power.

What is real power?

What exactly is a powerful person? Many people will say it is a person who has great power in the physical world, such as dictators, leaders of nations or commanders of great armies. Did people such as the Roman emperors, Genghis Kahn, Attila the Hun, Hitler, Stalin or Mao Zedong truly have great power— meaning personal power?

If you look at these people's state of mind, you will see that they were often willing to kill any number of other people, even their own people, in order to remain in power. Stalin and Mao both had millions of their own people executed, and this was not often a result of these people having actually threatened the leader. It was in most cases only a perceived threat, a threat in the mind of the leader himself.

What feels threatened? Only the ego. Why does the ego feel threatened? Because it has an existential fear, a fear it can never overcome. When you are willing to kill millions of people in order to destroy a perceived threat, you demonstrate that your mind is completely dominated by fear. The more people you are willing to kill, the more fear you have. A man who is eaten up by fear cannot be said to have personal power—regardless of the physical power he may command as leader of a system that has dehumanized those who seem to threaten the system.

A man who controls the world is still inferior to one who controls his own mind. True personal power means that in any situation you encounter on earth, you can choose your reaction freely. Instead of reacting through one of the games of the ego, you can react by being the open door for your I AM Presence and the power of God. This power may – as demonstrated by my so-called miracles – override the laws of nature that human

beings normally consider restrictions to their use of power—
and which are indeed restrictions to force-based power.

What does it take to be the open door for this true power?
It takes that you are free from the illusion of separation so
you do not perceive the situation through the filter of duality
and do not react as a separate individual. A separate individual
will often feel threatened, and it can react only by seeking to
destroy the threat—real or perceived.

Destroying any part of life can only take down the whole.
When you are not blinded by separation, you will be the open
door for actions or words that are aimed at raising the whole.
This might entail letting people kill your physical body in order
to let them outplay their ego games and make them more visible. It never, ever involves killing or forcing other people.
When you are in oneness, you can never destroy or put down
any part of life, for you know it is diminishing the whole—of
which you are an individual expression.

Why dualistic power will destroy itself

Those trapped in duality will believe the ego's illusion that they
are separate beings and that they are threatened by other separate beings. They will believe that if these other beings kill
them, it will be a loss for themselves. They believe it is "him or
me" and thus it is acceptable to kill those other beings in order
to preserve the separate self. They will even believe that they
can kill others without affecting themselves, something only a
separate being can believe.

When you are blinded by this illusion, you will believe that
power is the physical power you have in the material realm.
You will believe that power is the same as force, a force that
is stronger than any opposition and can force other people
to no longer be a threat to you. What have I explained in the

previous book? For every action, there is a reaction from the cosmic mirror.

When you send a force-based impulse into the cosmic mirror, you are in effect saying to the mirror that you want to live in a world where you – a separate being – are opposed by other separate beings. If all people are using force to get what they want, life becomes a giant competition to see who can generate the most force.

Each force-based impulse you send out will form an impulse that cycles through the four levels of the material universe before it comes back to you at the physical level. I realize this is not obvious because in most cases the impulse comes back lifetimes later when you have no conscious awareness of what you originally sent out. Nevertheless, when the impulse comes back to you, it will come back multiplied by the cosmic mirror. He who sows the wind will reap the whirlwind.

When the impulse comes back, you will encounter a situation where you feel physically threatened, and often you *will* indeed be physically threatened by other people. How can you avoid the threat? If you are still in the mindset of separation, you will think it can be done only by generating a force-based impulse that is powerful enough to repel the threat. What have you now done? You have sent a second force-based impulse into the mirror.

This impulse will also come back to you multiplied, and you now need to generate an even stronger impulse in order to repel it. As this goes on, there will come a point where you simply will not have the force to repel the return of your previous actions, and this will lead to your inevitable demise.

A lifestream such as Hitler had sent out many force-based impulses in past lives. When such an old impulse comes back, it does not come back directly to the physical level. It first comes back at the identity level, then the mental, then the emotional and then finally the physical. This means that most people will become aware of the impulse at one of the higher levels, meaning they will start to feel threatened before the impulse actually reaches the physical realm. This means the person has two options. It can change its consciousness and potentially avoid having the karmic impulse reach the physical level. Or it can seek to protect itself from the return by building a physical defense to repel the threat.

Hitler felt threatened from a young age and he attempted to turn the German nation into his personal bulwark against this threat. Even the armies of a large nation were not enough to generate a force-based impulse strong enough to turn back the physical consequences of what Hitler had personally sent out in past lives. By taking aggressive action on such a large scale, Hitler actually sent out an impulse that came back much sooner because of its force. At the moment he decided to start a war to conquer the world, his demise was a karmic certainty. He could have avoided this by not using his power in a destructive way, but that was not his choice and the result is proven for all to see. Of course, those who opposed Hitler had also generated force-based impulses in previous times, and the second world war was a giant web of these karmic connections that gave everyone an opportunity to see that no one can truly win by using force.

Escaping the arms race

The ego will never see that force-based power will eventually destroy itself. It will forever believe that if your opponent builds a stronger stone wall, you simply have to build a stronger cannon. The ego will continue in this "arms race" indefinitely. Why? Because it cannot see that as long as you are using force-based power, there will never be a final or absolute weapon or defense system. Let me explain this in more depth. As an illustration, consider a seesaw that you see on many playgrounds around the world. It is a beam that is balanced in the middle and where each end can move up and down. If you put a child on each end and if they have the same weight, they will balance each other. If one child is heavier, the other child will be lifted into the air. Alternatively, you can also move one child further away from the balancing point so that a lighter child can balance a heavier one.

Now transfer this principle to the situation between two nations that have armies of equal strength. How can you change the "balance of power?" The obvious way is to add more weight on your side, such as building a stronger stone fortification. The other option is to move the weight on your side farther from the center of the seesaw, perhaps even by extending your side of the beam so it becomes longer. You will see that nations have historically attempted to both create bigger armies and take their weapons more and more towards the extreme. Whatever you can do on your side, can in principle be done by your opponent on the other side.

If you look at this race for power from a superficial viewpoint, it would seem that the nation that is willing to add the most weight and that is willing to go further towards the extreme should be able to win and take over the earth. You have indeed seen very powerful empires that have attempted to take over the earth, but why have none of them succeeded? It is because of three factors:

•   In the material universe, everything has a cost. If you build a stronger stone wall, this takes resources and no individual and nation has unlimited resources. For example, a medieval city state may have forced its citizens to build a stronger stone wall around the city, but the people building the wall could not at the same time work the fields in order to feed themselves and the soldiers.

•   Anything that can be done with matter and energy can be counteracted by a different use of matter and energy. Although Newton's third law was developed to describe a specific scenario, the principle that for each action there is an equal and opposite reaction does explain that each action you could possibly take in the material realm can be counteracted by an opposing action. You may be able to take a decisive action on a temporary basis and win a victory. In the long run, someone will come up with a counter-move that will neutralize your advantage. You can gain a temporary advantage but never a permanent state of superiority.

•   As I have said, each force-based impulse will eventually be returned multiplied by the cosmic mirror.

Now consider what has happened on a world scale over the past century. During many previous centuries, people had attempted to build more powerful weapons and more powerful defenses. For example, during Medieval times, the main weapon was to build impenetrable stone walls. This lasted for thousands of years until gunpowder was invented. Suddenly a cannon set up at a safe distance could shatter even the strongest stone wall, and stone fortifications became obsolete almost overnight. This, of course, only led to a new race, namely to build more and more powerful cannons.

What we see is that in the linear arms race, people have attempted to add more weight on their side of the seesaw by building quantitatively larger armed forces and they have attempted to extend the beam by adding new and more powerful weapons. This arms race has been going on for thousands of years, and although it is still continuing, there is one thing that has changed the equation, namely the invention of nuclear weapons. Human beings now have weapons of such force that if used on a sufficient scale, the consequences would be such that instead of tipping the seesaw to the favor of one side, it would actually break the beam—meaning it would destroy the planet.

As a result, at least some nations have started to see the futility of the arms race and have seen the necessity of finding different ways to settle disagreements than through force. Take note that it took the threat of an ultimate force to get people to make this leap. Had nuclear weapons not been invented, there would not have been this shift in consciousness.

What does this have to do with you overcoming the ego? Even on a personal level, there is a limit to how much power you can exert. You have only a limited amount of physical power and you have only a limited ability to get others to fight for you. Many lifestreams will have to spend some lifetimes having to pursue the dream of gaining some form of ultimate personal power.

Many people are still trapped in this race, and when they leave embodiment and look at their lifetimes, they see how they did something that failed to give them power and they immediately think up something they could have done differently. Meaning they now have to take embodiment again to see if their latest theory will work.

For those open to this book, it should be easy to see that the ego's dream of having ultimate personal power simply can never be fulfilled. It is not a matter of a lifestream gradually (over many lifetimes) acquiring the knowledge, skills and power to make its vision come through. It is only a matter of how many lifetimes it takes before the Conscious You will have had enough of pursuing the ego's impossible dream and decides to simply walk away from the entire race for power.

Winning and losing

One factor that can become a detour for many people, keeping them trapped in the race for power longer than necessary, is that the ego can add the perspective that gaining power is not simply for its own sake but in order to win some kind of decisive victory. I will talk more about this when I talk about competition and also in the next book about ego dramas. If you think having personal power would allow you to win some kind of important victory, then you will think that the reason you have not yet won is that you have not attained enough power. It then follows logically that you cannot quit the race for power until you have won the victory.

Getting out of this ego game requires two things. One is that the Conscious You comes to understand what I have said above, namely that a final or decisive outcome can never be achieved through earthly power. The other is that the Conscious You begins to see that everything you do on earth has a price, namely that it eats up your energy and your attention.

Look at some of the powerful leaders seen throughout history. They first spend an enormous amount of energy and attention on getting into a position of power. In some cases they did manage to do something that was a decisive step on a temporary basis. For example, some of the Roman emperors won decisive battles that gave them a great sense of victory and power, but who cares about these victories today?

Even if you do win some victory, it is inevitable that you will come to a point where all of your energy and attention is consumed by keeping up your power. Just look at how many leaders spend the better part of their lives defending their position against all kinds of threats, often only perceived threats. There simply comes a point in a lifestream's evolution where the Conscious You looks at this, sees the vanity and futility of it and decides that it wants something more than earthly power can give it.

Spiritual people and power games

Obviously, most spiritually minded people have overcome the desire for having the physical power to destroy their enemies. However, some are still caught up in the desire to destroy an enemy and are willing to join an army and fight for their country or a cause they think is desirable from a spiritual viewpoint. Can there ever be a true spiritual cause that necessitates the killing or forcing of human beings? In the eyes of the ego there can, as witnessed by the Crusades, the Inquisition, modern terrorism and many other examples of people feeling that the use of force was justified by God himself. Again, how many lifetimes will it take before the Conscious You realizes that this is an illusion and simply walks away from it?

I will address these ego dramas in greater depth in the coming book, but what I want to talk about here is that many spiritual people have a desire to acquire not physical power but psychic power, the power of the mind. Many spiritual people go through an awakening and realize that this world has a lot of problems that are caused by a lack of awareness. They correctly see that the only real solution is to raise the spiritual awareness of the population, but then they are deceived by their egos into thinking this means everyone should be converted into following a specific spiritual teaching or guru. As they try to convert other people and are disappointed by their lack of response, they can be deceived into thinking that if only they could produce some kind of visible phenomenon, people would be convinced that they are right and everyone would see the value of the spiritual path as defined by their teachings. This now sends them into another power race, namely the quest for psychic power.

As I have said, everything in the material world comes with a price tag. Whatever you focus your mind upon will eat up your attention and psychic energy. The more you focus your attention upon something, the more psychic energy you feed into it. This energy will eventually begin to form a vortex that spins, and once a vortex has formed in your energy field, it will act as a magnet that pulls more energy into itself. As long as you focus your attention on the topic, you will feed energy into the vortex.

Now comes the subtle distinction. You can actually build such a strong vortex of psychic energy that it can eventually have effects even on physical matter. As you might have seen with some people, they can move objects, bend spoons or produce other such phenomena. There are even some who have used black magic to acquire the power to kill others or overpower their minds with thought alone. The simple fact is that this is entirely ego-driven and *never* comes from the Christ mind.

The Christ mind does want people to awaken but not through force. The Christ mind is ready to help every human being raise its consciousness to the next level, but the Christ does not seek to force people. It waits until people are ready, and then it offers its assistance. What will it take for people to be ready? As I said in the previous book, it takes that they have a certain amount of experiences in the material world and now want more than matter has to offer.

Even if you had great psychic powers and could produce visible phenomena, it would not have a positive effect. First of all, if you understand what I have said about perception filters, you will see that people can deny anything. A skeptic or materialist will always be able to find an explanation for explaining away any phenomena you might produce. Secondly, even if people are converted by such phenomena, it will not mean they are ready for the true spiritual path. They may follow a certain outer teaching or guru, but that is not the same as being ready to truly raise their consciousness and overcome the ego.

Back to the subtle distinction. It is indeed possible to produce certain phenomena through the Christ mind. I did perform many miracles, even many more than recorded in the scriptures. You might notice several things by reading the scriptures carefully. You will notice that I would ask a person before healing him or her. It was the person's belief that was the open door for performing a healing, never me imposing myself upon others as an external force. There were many people who were not healed because they were not ready or willing. You will also notice that I often asked the people who were healed not to tell anyone. In retrospect, this was naive because people will always talk, but it does show that a true master does not produce phenomena to convince people who are not ready. Take note that I often confronted the scribes and Pharisees, but I only did so with words, not with miracles.

When the Christ mind performs a phenomenon that is beyond the laws of nature, it is not you – as a separate self – doing this. You have – at least temporarily – overcome separation and attained a degree of oneness with the Christ mind. You are not the doer, you are the open door for the Christ mind to act through you. In order to attain this, you must overcome all of the desires of the ego-based self. You are completely neutral and you are letting the Christ mind decide what to do—if anything. If nothing happens, you are completely at peace with this because you know that with your outer mind, you cannot produce any phenomenon that is worthy. Take note that you can actually have two people who both perform a phenomenon, such as healing someone. One person is driven by an ego-based desire while the other is in the Christ mind. By only looking at their outer actions, you will not be able to tell the difference. As you acquire Christ discernment, you will be able to read the vibration and thereby the intent behind it.

If you look at yourself honestly and discover that in your being is still remnants of this desire to convert or impress other people with psychic abilities, then it would be wise to take a closer look at this. Regardless of the clever disguise and the elaborate justifications, this can *only* come from the ego. Why? Because when you are in the Christ mind, you have no forethought, you have no plans. Why do you need to plan ahead when you know you are not the doer? If you are letting God be the doer, you are literally witnessing what God is doing as it is happening. If something is not produced by your mind, how can there be forethought?

There can be a general thought about what it takes to be the open door for the power of God, and this is valid as far as it helps you follow the path towards overcoming the ego. Even this can be taken by the ego and turned into a new force-based impulse of changing the minds of other people. Go back and read what I said in the previous book about free will and allowing people to walk their own path. You will see that in order to be the Living Christ in embodiment, you must overcome *all* desires to force the minds of other people. As long as you have a subtle desire to change the minds of others, you cannot be the fully open door for the Christ mind.

The non-power game

As you see many people playing the game of seeking to acquire personal power, you also see many more people playing the game that forms the opposite dualistic polarity, namely the game of denying their power. These are people who are playing the game of defining themselves as essentially powerless beings who are the helpless victims of circumstances beyond their control. You even find many such people in spiritual movements where they are the passive followers of a guru that they have elevated to a superior status and now worship as an idol who is fundamentally beyond themselves and holds the key to their salvation.

Here is another subtle distinction. We have in many of our teachings talked about the fact that there is a small group of people on earth who are what we call fallen beings, meaning beings who have not only fallen into the duality consciousness but who did so in a previous sphere. [For more about this, see *Healing Mother Earth*.] When you look at history and also at the world today, it is clear that the worst examples of abuses of power are perpetrated by these beings. This has set up a certain dynamic that spiritual seekers need to recognize.

A new lifestream will take some time before it is able to exercise power. Many of the people you see on earth are relatively new lifestreams and they see themselves as powerless beings because they have not yet learned how to use their power. They *are* in a sense powerless beings. This is, of course, a condition that is greatly encouraged by the fallen beings who want to control the population and make them tools in their personal quest for power.

Most spiritual seekers are older lifestreams who have learned something about power but who have also seen and experienced the abuses of power precipitated by the fallen beings. Many spiritual seekers have started to see the fallacy of such abuses of power, and that is actually one reason they are attracted to spiritual teachings as a tool to raise the earth beyond the abuses of power. Even spiritual – and especially religious – teachings have been influenced by the fallen beings and used as tools for pacifying people by getting them to deny their power.

There are many false gurus in the world, and with "false" I mean people who have learned how to use their power to get other people to deny their own power. These spiritual leaders want to have followers, and in order to keep you as a follower they must get you to deny your inner power, making you think you are dependent upon *their* power. In contrast, a true teacher is seeking to help you discover and liberate the power of God within you so you come to the point of no longer needing the teacher.

Many spiritual seekers are ready to consciously exercise the power of God within them, which is why I, in the first book in this series, [*The Mystical Teachings of Jesus*] talk about 10,000 people who are ready to claim their Christhood and millions more who can claim it in this lifetime. Many spiritual people have looked at the abuses of power precipitated by the fallen beings and decided that they never want to be guilty of such abuse of power. This realization comes from the Christ mind, but these people have then been deceived by their egos into jumping to the opposite extreme and deciding that in order to avoid abusing power they simply will refuse to have any kind of power in society.

The entire point of spiritual growth is to work toward the Christ consciousness where you become an open door for your I AM Presence to express itself through you. This does not necessarily mean that you have to have a powerful position in society but then again, it might mean that you do something publicly. Regardless of what is in your personal divine plan, the only way to fulfill that plan is to become an open door, which means that you do not – with the outer mind – put any limitations on what your I AM Presence and the Christ mind can do through you.

In order to become the open door, you need to build Christ discernment so you realize that you have more than two options. It is not so that you must either exercise power as the fallen beings do or you must refuse to have power. You can find the Middle Way of exercising power by being the open door for the power of God whereby you are not the doer.

There is a fine, but very real, distinction between the dualistic polarities of the ego and being the Christ in action. When you see life through the perception filter of the ego, it seems as if you are either the doer or you must do nothing. You either exercise power as a separate individual or you refuse to have power. When you grow towards Christhood, you can go beyond the dualistic scale and begin to exercise power through the Christ mind instead of through the separate mind. This is very much needed if the earth is to be raised out of the grip of the fallen beings who today define almost every aspect of how people look at life.

The trick is that you will not acquire perfect discernment instantaneously. You will acquire is through practice, which means you will sometimes make mistakes. It doesn't matter that you make mistakes if you recognize this because then you turn it into a victory. Having believed in a dualistic lie does not matter once you have come to see through it and used it to build Christ discernment. This is the most supreme responsibility of any true spiritual seeker: the responsibility to discern based on the Christ mind. All of us who have ascended from earth have been fooled by the subtlety of the duality consciousness but we have also learned how to turn this into stepping stones for progress.

The Christ mind is neither in one nor in the other dualistic polarity. The Christ mind can in every situation show people that there is something beyond the dualistic mind. *That* is real power because it is the power to give people a real choice instead of the false choice of thinking they have to choose between two dualistic polarities. If you want to help raise the earth into The Golden Age of Saint Germain, become an open door for *that* power and then dare to exercise it in all situations you encounter.

8 | CONTROL GAMES

Control games can be seen as one aspect of power games. However, raw power games can easily form a self-reinforcing spiral that leads to more and more extreme expressions of force. For example, many leaders who abuse power gradually become so extreme that the outcome is a war in which they either destroy others or are themselves destroyed. We can say that a raw power game is one that causes you to lose control, eventually leading to your own destruction.

A control game is where you express power in a way that is more restrained—controlled. This means people can express power for a longer period of time, but the price they pay is that they must continually seek to control others, even their own people. When you set out to control others, the first person to be controlled is yourself.

Why is this so? What does it mean to control others? There is, of course, raw control through physical force. As history bears out, control through direct physical force is very difficult to attain and even more difficult to maintain over a long period of time. Say a dictator of one country occupies another country. How can he control the citizens of the occupied country? He could throw them all in jail, but then what would be the point of occupying the country? He could assign three soldiers to physically guard each person 24 hours a day, but does he have that kind of resources?

The only practical way to control others is to get into their minds and get them to accept a certain world view, a certain mental box. Joseph Stalin had great physical power to arrest and execute people, and it is estimated he killed 21 million people in the Soviet Union. He realized, however, that he could not physically control every person so he instituted "Red Terror," a campaign where he used special forces to randomly kill people or make them disappear. The result was that no one felt safe and eventually everyone decided to not resist and accept the mental box which said that communism could not be overthrown and that Stalin was the supreme, undisputed leader. Stalin had broken people's resistance, but this happened in the psyches of the people.

What did Stalin have to do in order to accomplish this goal? He first had to create a mental box defining the Soviet Union as a totalitarian regime where there was no law except what one man – Stalin himself – defined. In order to do this, he first had to believe in that mental box, meaning he was the first prisoner of it. Most of the time Stalin did not feel like a prisoner because he could divert his attention with the feeling of having ultimate power. I can assure you that, especially towards the end of his reign, Stalin started feeling trapped and confined but now saw no way out. He knew that if he relaxed his iron grip, a spiral would start that would eventually cause the entire Soviet system to unravel. He had to keep himself and the people in the mental box in order to maintain the system, which had now come to own him and use him as a tool.

Why control cannot last forever

You will see that the Soviet leaders who came after Stalin realized he had gone too far in his abuse of power. They gradually sought to lift the threat of execution and imprisonment, and several leaders thought they could do this and still keep the Soviet Union intact. The last Soviet leader, Gorbachev, even thought he could give western-style freedoms and that this would improve the economy and people's standard of living while maintaining the basic Soviet system.

What Gorbachev and others did not understand was that the people had not chosen communism, and they stayed in it only as long as the mental box that controlled them was intact. That mental box was created through the uncompromising threat of death, and it was only the fear of death that controlled the people. As soon as Soviet leaders began relaxing the threat and the people began realizing the threat was no longer as severe, they wanted more freedom, then more freedom— and this continued until the Soviet system simply could not be maintained. The mental box created by Lenin and Stalin had been dismantled.

Why did this happen? It happened partly because, as explained in the discourse on power games, anything that is based on force will generate a counterforce from the cosmic mirror. You need to use more and more force to simply maintain the system and this will eventually exceed the resources available.

The promise made by Lenin was that communism would be a worker's paradise where all people would have a comfortable standard of living. Because the system was based on force, it inevitably defined itself an external enemy and that – combined with the extreme paranoia of Stalin – meant the Soviet Union was locked in an arms race from the very beginning. Had there not been the need to divert greater and greater resources to the military, the Soviet Union might have provided a comfortable standard of living—for a time. Because the system was based on force from the beginning, it simply could not exist without an external enemy. Communism, from Marx's day, defined itself in opposition to Capitalism and locked itself into a dualistic struggle that would eat up its resources and invalidate its central promise of affluence for all workers.

The other aspect is that any force-based system goes against the very driving force of life itself, namely the drive to become more. People have an inherent drive for freedom and you either suppress this brutally, as Stalin did, or you will see that it will eventually overthrow every force-based system.

What is it that controls people?

Now, it is not my aim here to discourse on world history but to give you a foundation for understanding how the ego controls you. Stalin could not have physically killed all people in the Soviet Union, but he did not have to because all people believed in the threat that anyone who resisted would be killed. What controlled the people was not the actual physical apparatus that could kill some people. If all people had revolted at once, that apparatus would have been neutralized. What truly controlled people was a mechanism in their minds. The conclusion is that the basis for any kind of control is to get into people's minds and block their connection to the Christ mind.

What have I said in the previous discourses and in my other teachings? You are not a human being limited to this physical body and the material world. You are a spiritual being who can easily exist without your current physical body and the life you have built in this lifetime. Once you realize and accept who you are, nothing on earth will be able to control you because you will know that whatever they might do to your body – such as nail you to a cross – they will never be able to do anything to your mind—for you have taken control of your mind.

Why don't you have full control of your mind right now? Because there is a division in your mind, you are a house divided against itself. This division was created because you entered the duality consciousness and created two aspects of the ego, which as I say in the first book led to the creation of two spirits. [For more on the creation of such spirits, see the book *Flowing With the River of Life*.] These spirits were created here in the material world and they believe their survival depends on specific conditions in the material world. The spirits want you to stay within certain boundaries in this world, they want you to hang on to certain conditions in the material world as if your life depended on it.

How is it possible for other people to control you? They can do so only because they have something inside your psyche that they can use to make you feel attached to certain conditions here on earth. If you were willing to give up and leave behind anything and everything you have on earth, how could any power on earth control you? That is why I said that only those willing to give up everything could follow me into Christhood.

You can be controlled when you feel that here is something on earth that you simply cannot exist without. Someone makes the threat to take away what you think you cannot live without, yet he also makes the promise that if you submit to certain restrictions, you can keep your treasure. If you truly think you cannot live without it, you will indeed submit. What is it in you that feels it cannot live without something on earth? If you are a spiritual being, how could you ever come to feel this way? The magic of our teachings about the Conscious You is that once you realize and experience that you are pure awareness, you directly experience that your existence does not depend on anything on earth. This can then open you up to seeing that what feels it cannot live without something on earth is not you but a spirit that exists inside your energy field. This spirit was created based on certain conditions on earth and it truly cannot live without them.

The spirit is a perception filter, like colored glasses. As long as you do not realize that you are simply looking at life through the perception filter of a spirit, you will think that the spirit's fear is your fear. When you realize that you are a Conscious You that is pure spirit, you will know that you will not die when you lose your earthly "life." That is when you will be willing to follow my call that those who seek to save their lives shall lose them whereas those who are willing to lose their lives in order to follow me into oneness will find eternal life.

You already have eternal life. The spirits in your being can never see this, for they can never attain eternal life. They are mortal and they can never become immortal. The Conscious You is already immortal and simply needs to realize this. You realize this only by coming to see the spirits for what they are, seeing that you are not these spirits and then consciously letting them die. This is what the spirits, the ego and all dark forces will do anything in their power to prevent. They will do anything to prevent you from being able to say with me: "The prince of this world cometh and has nothing in me."

Spiritual people and control games

The most subtle effect of the ego is that it makes you see life through the perception filter of a mortal spirit without you realizing that the way you see life is a distorted vision. You believe that your existence depends on certain conditions in the material realm. It now follows that in order to preserve your existence – the basic survival instinct – you must seek to maintain those conditions in the material world. How can you do this? By seeking to control something in this world. You are now condemned to the prison of seeking to control something in this world. What is it you must control? Here are the main things:

• Some people think they have to control God, and most mainstream religions are basically designed to give people the sense that through their religion they have some control over God.

• Some people believe they have to control nature, and modern science and technology is very much affected by this drive to discover the laws of nature in order to control nature.

• Some people believe they have to control other people and there is almost no limit to the philosophies and schemes that people will come up with in order to control others. Spiritual teachings, even ascended master teachings, can be used by the ego in its attempt to control others.

Let us now look at the realism of thinking that a human being could control God, the laws of nature and other people. As I said, what seeks to attain this control is a spirit that lives inside your energy field. This spirit was created in the material world, and it will never be able to fathom that its attempts at control are doomed from the beginning. Only the Conscious

You can fathom this and it can do so only through a direct, inner experience where you intuitively see the futility of seeking to control anything. Let us look at the three factors:

• **God.** The ego thinks it can define God and it also thinks it can control what it has defined. The Conscious You can experience the Presence of God and this will give you a frame of reference for seeing that God is completely beyond form. That which is beyond form simply cannot be controlled by anything in the world of form. God is no respecter of persons. When you have this experience, you can see the futility of the spirits who use religion, even ascended master teachings, in an attempt to control God. It will be an enormous relief for you to let go of this subtle attempt to control God and it will open you up to experiencing the unconditional love that God and all ascended masters have for you. When you experience that love from within your self, why would you need to control anything outside your self?

• **Nature.** The very purpose of the laws of nature is to provide human beings with a frame of reference that allows them to physically see that there is something they cannot control through duality. In medieval times people believed the earth was the center of the universe and that it functioned only to serve them. As science discovers how vast and complex the universe is, does it not become increasingly obvious that this expansive universe is not created to serve human beings on earth and that its basic functions will never be controllable from this little planet? Again, only the Conscious You can have this Aha experience.

• **Other people.** What could potentially make it possible for you to control another person? It is that you have free will and you can make the choice to try to control another. If you have free will, would the other person not also have free will? If so, then you will not actually be able to control another person. You may be able to get another person to choose to submit to your control but the other person could at any time choose to change that choice. Again, the ego will never see this, but the Conscious You can indeed see it. Giving up the desire to control others will lift an immense burden from you, setting you free to live a life where you seek to control nothing and where nothing controls you. As long as you seek to control another human being, you will never attain control over your own mind. Only self-control can give you the inner peace that the ego seeks through controlling the external world.

Why control is possible but cannot be maintained

Let us now take this to a more subtle level. As we have explained in other teachings, the material universe is meant to give you certain experiences until you feel you have had enough of them and move on. As we have also explained, these experiences take place inside your own mind and it is here you will decide when you have had enough and want to move on.

This means that the material universe has two functions. One is to give you any experience you desire to have, even the experience that you can control God, nature and other people. In reality, as I have explained, you cannot control these circumstances, but through a spirit created for this purpose, you can indeed have the experience – an illusion, but an illusion that seems very real from inside your perception filter – that you can control God, nature and other people.

This means that once you step inside the perception filter of such a spirit, you become a self-fulfilling prophecy. You are not actually controlling God, but it seems like you are. How is this feeling attained? Because the spirit blocks out all evidence that would question the illusion that you are in control. You literally see only what confirms your illusion and you are able to ignore or dismiss any evidence to the contrary. This is why any perception filter – *any* perception filter – becomes a closed mental box that imprisons the Conscious You until you look at the filter (the spirit) and see that it is not real and it is not you.

Now, while the universe is designed to give you any experience you want, it is not designed to give you this experience indefinitely. You are an extension of God's Being and God will allow itself to be imprisoned in a mortal form, but it does not want to be imprisoned forever. The material universe does have certain factors that will eventually begin to intrude upon your illusion that you are in perfect control.

I have already described these as the counterforce generated by any force-based impulse you send out, but in terms of control games, I would like to point to the factor of human beings. However, let us look at all three factors:

•   In a sense **God** is the easiest factor to control because God has given you free will and God will not force itself upon you. Once human beings have created the image of the remote God who is not here on earth, there is not much God can do to shatter this image. The ascended masters can indeed send representatives to earth who demonstrate that there is a higher form of consciousness, but people can easily ignore or discredit this through their perception filters.

- **Nature**. While people have indeed used modern technology to build defensive walls between themselves and nature, there is not presently, nor will there ever be, a technological way to completely control nature. Natural disasters are simply the return of the force-based impulses that people have collectively sent out. It is technologically possible to control a force like a hurricane, but doing so would use up so many resources that it would be impractical. Wouldn't it just be so much easier to purify the collective consciousness of misqualified energy, meaning the nature spirits do not become so overburdened that they have to release the energy this way [See *Healing Mother Earth*]? While it is still easy to build the perception that you can control nature, nature will only comply for a time and it has some pretty obvious ways to make its non-compliance known.

- **People**. Obviously, the easiest way to build a sense of control is to build the illusion that you can control other people. This is also the illusion that can last the longest and be the most difficult to shatter. Presently, the vast majority of people on this planet are playing along with the illusion that a small elite can control the population.

What did I come to demonstrate 2,000 years ago? I came to demonstrate that nothing in this world can prevent an individual from attaining the Christ consciousness and that nothing can control a Christed being. What I need today – and one motivation for giving these ego discourses – is for millions of people to awaken to their potential to do what I did by refusing to submit to the mechanisms of control found in this world. The spiritual people of today are the only ones who can rise above these mechanisms of control and demonstrate to the general population that you do not have to live within the mental boxes defined by a small elite of fallen beings. For you to fulfill this potential, you first have to rise above any desire you have to control God, nature and other people.

Control games cancel out spirituality

What did I say was the basis for control? Stalin could not physically kill every person in the Soviet Union—and if he had done so, what would have given him a sense of power? He did not have to kill them all, for it was enough that they feared that they could be killed. What controls you is fear—the fear of loss.

If you look at the world, you will see that some people are not open to the spiritual path while a few are. What is the difference? The fear of loss is unbearable, you simply cannot live with it. We might say that the forces who want to control you face an inescapable dilemma. In order to control you, they must induce the fear of loss in your being. In order to continue to control you, they must enable you to reduce this fear to a level you can live with. They must both create a problem and offer you relief from it.

How is this accomplished? In reality, the forces that seek to control people are not facing a dilemma. They operate in the field of duality, and in duality there are always two polarities. All these forces have to do, is to get you to accept one of the subtle, serpentine illusions that spring from the duality consciousness. Once you accept such an illusion, you will – without being aware of this – create two spirits. One spirits is created from the fear of loss, the fear of death and annihilation. The other is created from the illusion that by living up to certain conditions on earth, you can escape death. Look at the three factors mentioned above:

• **God.** One spirit fears God as an angry and judgmental being in the sky who will send you to hell. Another spirit believes that if you follow the prescripts of a particular religion on earth, the angry God will reward you with eternal life in heaven. These two spirits do not cancel out each other so you are still trapped in the middle. You will never actually escape the fear of God's punishment, but by focusing on the second spirit, you can live with the fear of loss.

• **Nature.** One spirit fears that you can die at any moment from natural disasters. Another spirit convinces you that it will happen to someone else, and thus you can live with the fear although you will never be able to live without the fear.

• **People.** One spirit makes you fear what other people will do, that they will betray you, leave you or let you down. Another spirit convinces you that through some scheme or other you will be able to control them and prevent this. Again, you can live with the fear.

What is the difference between those who have awakened to the spiritual path and those who have not? Those who have not awakened are still trapped in the fragile balance between the two spirits, the one that induces fear and the one that promises to relieve it. Those who are open to the spiritual path have started to doubt that this scenario is right, they have started to doubt the spirit that offers relief and they now acknowledge their fear.

It is a simple fact that most of the people who awaken to the spiritual path do so out of fear. They begin to acknowledge the existential fear of death – their angst – and they begin to grapple for a better solution than the "normality" offered by the second spirit. They begin to look for a real way out.

This will almost inevitably launch people into a somewhat tumultuous, even schizophrenic phase, in which they seek to overcome the fear of death without fully understanding the dynamic of the two spirits. That is why their egos are often able to take them into a blind alley where they simply use the spiritual teachings they have found – even the teachings of the ascended masters – as a way to seek the control that the ego thinks is the only way to alleviate fear. Let us look at how this works:

• **God.** People will think that because they have found this sophisticated spiritual teaching or guru, they now have the ultimate way to control God and get him to give them a break so they can be saved without having to do the hard work of unraveling their own psychology and dismissing the ego and its illusions.

• **Nature.** People will think that they now have such a powerful spiritual practice that they can avert natural disasters, at least for them personally. Or they will think that because they are so spiritual, God will grant them a favor and spare them from what befalls others.

• **People.** Most spiritual people will go through a phase where they seek to control other people by using their spiritual teaching. This is usually done by using the teaching to induce fear or play upon people's existing fears.

I am not saying this to blame anyone. All of us who have ascended have gone through these phases and eventually came to see the futility of trying to control anything. Even when you do attain a certain degree of control, you will actually realize that this does not remove your fear. Why not? Where is *your* fear located? It is located inside *your* mind. How will you overcome your *inner* fear by controlling *outer* circumstances?

Think about this simple logic and allow the Conscious You to be free to experience the reality of it. What is actually the core of fear? It is that you are not in control of your destiny, your life experience. What can take away this control? To the ego, only something external to yourself.

To the ego, it is perfectly logical that if something external to yourself can take away your control, then the way to overcome your fear of losing control is to seek to control that external something. The Conscious You is capable of experiencing the fallacy of this. It is capable of realizing that your destiny is not dependent upon anything external to you.

Your destiny is dependent upon how you react to what is external to you, it is dependent upon what happens inside your mind. You do have the potential to take control of what happens inside your mind by seeing that you are a Conscious You, that you are pure awareness and as such you cannot be divided. Something external can control you only when there is a division in your being, namely two spirits. But you are not those spirits and can at any time rise above them and simply leave them behind.

The ego and the spirits will scream at you that you cannot simply leave them behind, and they will give you all kinds of subtle reasons for this. How do you become free of this control? Only when the Conscious You realizes – consciously – that all of the reasons are invalid because since you are pure spirit your existence depends on nothing on earth. Letting go of something on earth can never be a loss to the Conscious You, it can only be a gain because it brings you one step closer to freedom.

Take note of a subtle distinction. As I said in the previous book, free will gives you the right to have any experience you want for as long as you want. Some lifestreams have a desire to experience life as separate beings and in order to have this experience, they need to experience life through the perception filters of dualistic spirits. It is possible that a person who still has not had enough of that experience could pick up this book and read to this point. If so, the spirits of that person will come up with very sophisticated arguments for why the person should reject what I am saying.

Truly, if you have not had enough of experiencing life as a separate being, those arguments would be valid. If you want to continue having the experience as a separate being, you should indeed ignore my teachings, and you might even want to go on a crusade to prove me wrong in all kinds of ways.

The basic law for how the ascended masters work is this: When the student is ready, the teacher appears. It is also an inevitable consequence of the material universe that when we put a teaching into a book, it is possible that people can find the book before they are ready for it—at least at the level of the outer mind. If that applies to you, please do ignore the teaching until at some later point you might want to come back for a second look.

I trust that those who are indeed ready, and who are ready to acknowledge that they are ready, will see that the only way to overcome the desire to control others is to overcome fear. The only way to overcome the fear of loss is to overcome the illusion that you are a mortal being whose existence depends on anything on earth. I trust they will see that fear of loss is built into the separate self, the dualistic spirits. A spirit is created based on conditions in the material world and nothing in the material world is permanent. The spirit has a fear of loss that can never be alleviated. Even if you were able to control everything on earth, your fear of loss would remain.

Some people overcome the fear of losing something by actually losing it and then experiencing that they still exist and that they can still find some meaning in life. The point of any spiritual teaching is that the Conscious You does not need to have a physical experience of losing something. It can overcome the fear of loss by separating itself from the spirit that generates it. You can actually attain spiritual growth without having traumatic physical experiences.

You do not have to lose everything you have on earth in order to follow Christ. You do have to *be willing* to lose everything on earth in order to follow me. If there is anything on earth that you think you cannot leave behind in order to follow me, then you are not ready to follow me. You are not ready to give up the spirit that gives you the life experience that you are dependent upon something on earth. It is only by completely giving up the desire to control anything on earth that you gain the ability to control what really matters: yourself.

I am the living Christ. I do not want to force you into the total freedom of oneness. I simply stand ever-ready to offer you that freedom when you decide that you want it more than you want anything on earth.

❧

People create
their own suffering
by their own resistance
to growth—the harder the resistance,
the more intense the suffering.

❧

9 | COMPETITION AND COMPARISON GAMES

I am hoping you are beginning to see the basic dynamic that guides life on earth. The Creator has given you self-awareness and free will. You grow in self-awareness by exercising your free will. You have two basic options for making choices, one is choices based on the awareness that all life is one, which I call the Christ consciousness. The other is to make choices based on the illusion that you are a separate being, which I call the consciousness of anti-christ, the consciousness of death.

Contrary to what many religious and spiritual people believe, the deeper reality is that God has given you free will so there is nothing inherently wrong in choosing to go into separation. God does not judge you or condemn you to hell for going into separation. The reason is that God's purpose for giving you free will is that this is the only way you can grow in self-awareness, and experiencing life as a separate being can expand your self-awareness in the long run. However, going into separation means limiting your self-awareness so this expansion takes place only after you awaken from the illusion that you are a separate being. Going into separation means that you think: "I am *this* identity." After some time, you will realize: "Oh, I am not this identity; I am more than this identity." This realization is what leads to a growth in self-awareness. You ascend when you realize that you are more than any identity that could possibly be created on earth.

From this perspective, there is nothing inherently wrong with the ego and the ego games. The ego is simply what makes it seem believable to you that you are a separate being and that there is still something you want to do and experience on earth. The ego games are what give you the experience that you are a particular kind of separate being who has something to do or experience on earth. We can compare this to an actor who puts on a costume and make-up and then psychologically gets into character before going on stage.

Take note that an actor does not forget that he or she is not the character portrayed on the stage. When the play is over, the actor simply takes off the costume and make-up and returns to his or her normal sense of self. The difference between acting and taking embodiment is that you do not retain the memory that you are a spiritual being who has simply taken on a role. You go into separation by the Conscious You literally entering into a separate self, and once it is in there, everything it sees affirms that you are a separate being. You will forget that you are a spiritual being and think you are a mortal being. You can awaken from this forgetting at any time, but you have to awaken and this is not as simple as taking off a costume.

What now needs to be added is that there exist what we have called fallen beings who have chosen to not only go into separation but to rebel against God's purpose and plan for having all beings grow in self-awareness. They have built a separate self which believes it knows better than the Creator and that its mission is to prove that the Creator made a mistake by giving all self-aware beings free will. These beings have used their free will to decide that they want to take away the free will of all other beings.

As a sincere spiritual student there comes a point where you can go no higher on the path until you acknowledge the existence of the fallen beings and how they are using the ego and its games for the purpose of preventing you from awakening from the illusion of separation. If you take the fallen beings out of the equation, you would still have an ego and the ego would still be playing certain games. You would be identified with this ego, but after having had a certain amount of experiences, your built-in drive to become more would make you wonder if there is not more to life than what you experience through a particular ego game. Without the fallen beings, it would simply take a certain amount of time before you would start awakening from the ego-based sense of identity.

What the fallen beings are trying to do is to delay this awakening indefinitely. For the vast majority of lifestreams, they cannot prevent it from happening, but on a planet like earth, they have been quite successful in delaying the awakening for the lifestreams embodying here. How have they done this? By either taking advantage of the natural ego games and taking them further towards the extreme, or by creating entirely new ego games. This always follows the basic pattern of inducing a certain fear or problem through one spirit and then inducing the illusion that you can alleviate the fear or solve the problem through another spirit. With this in mind, let me give you one example of how this works.

You are not good enough

In a distant past, way before recorded history, there was a phase where the inhabitants of earth had started going into separation in increasing numbers. They had not yet taken the collective consciousness to the low point that allowed fallen beings to start embodying on this planet. Back then you had the ego game of people who saw themselves as separate beings competing against each other in order to win. What you saw back then was more like the kind of competition you see today in the highest form of sportsmanship. It was what is embodied in the Olympic spirit, which in its pure form is meant to bring people together in friendly competition in order to build a common bond even a sense of team spirit. Each person was competing to be as good as possible at a certain task but never sought to destroy the abilities of other people.

When the fallen beings started embodying on earth, they immediately started using the competition game in order to accomplish the goal of delaying people's awakening from separation. They did this by inducing the illusion that God is an angry and judgmental God and that some people are not good enough in the eyes of God, meaning they will be punished and sent to hell.

Those who believed in this image of God now created two spirits in their beings, one that truly believed in the angry God and one that offered relief or escape from the wrath of this non-existent God. When it came to people who were already into the competition games, this had the following effect. One spirit told them that they were not good enough in the eyes of God, and another told them that if they were better than others, then God would have to accept them, for he could not send everyone to hell.

What had instantly been accomplished by the fallen beings was to turn the game of friendly competition into a very unfriendly game of seeking to compensate for your own deficit by being better than others. Which then very easily was taken into the game of seeking to raise yourself up by aggressively putting other people down.

The core of comparison

I have said that in the ideal scenario a new lifestream starts out with a point-like sense of self but also with an inner sense of connection to something greater than itself. That something is the I AM Presence, but for a long time the new lifestream will have no conscious vision of the Presence. It acquires this vision by expanding its sense of self, by raising its consciousness.

How does a new lifestream expand its sense of self? It does so by interacting with the material world *and* by referring all of its interactions to its inner connection. This means the new lifestream has a sense that there is a reality beyond the material world, meaning nothing in this world is ultimately real. It knows it is not a product of the material world but came from somewhere else. It cannot come to identify itself with and as its own creation but sees its creation in this world as a springboard to expanding its sense of self.

A new lifestream grows by expressing its creative abilities and comparing the result to what it feels within. As it has created something, it looks at its creation and evaluates how it feels compared to its inner sense of connectedness. It basically considers (although for some time this is not done consciously) the question: "How well does my material creation express who I really am?" A lifestream that is not lost in separation has en internal frame of reference for evaluating all of its creative efforts. It is not really creating in order to achieve or own something in this world but in order to expand its sense of self.

Once a being steps into separation, it forgets its inner connection. It can no longer have an internal frame of reference. It might have a valuable frame of reference in the form of an outer spiritual teaching, but this is still something outside itself. If you are the one defining a person's frame of reference, you can exert an incredible degree of control over that person. The fallen beings knew this before they even came to earth so from the moment they came here they started to completely redefine every thought system on earth in order to pervert it to their own ends.

The ascended masters can counteract that by giving new spiritual teachings, even direct revelation. The moment a teaching enters the material realm, the fallen beings will seek to destroy, counteract or pervert it. They know full well that their control over the population depends on their ability to control what people use as a frame of reference. The bottom line being that they must maintain a situation where people use an external frame of reference.

The very core of competition is comparison, but the core of comparison is that you compare yourself to other people and you do so based on a standard defined in this world. Take note of what I said about a new lifestream that has not lost its connection to the Presence. It does not compare itself to other people because it always looks within to evaluate its creative efforts. It does not need an external standard in this world because it has an internal standard that is beyond this world. Even a being with a limited self-awareness is difficult to control.

The core of comparison is the external standard, a standard that is defined in this world. Very few people have a strong enough ego to create their own standard, and for most their personal standard is highly affected by an external standard created over time. This standard was not created by one fallen being, for even a fallen being does not have an ego big enough to single-handedly create such a standard. The standards that reside in the collective consciousness have been created by many fallen beings (both in and out of embodiment) and they have been created over time.

This explains why it is difficult for any individual to see through and expose such standards, and this explain why you need the Christ mind and outer teachings given from the Christ mind by the ascended masters. You can use these teachings as an outer frame of reference until you regain and strengthen your inner connection to your Christ self and I AM Presence and no longer need an outer teaching.

The black whole of competition

Now take note of why competition games can delay your awakening from duality for a very long time. You have come to see yourself as a separate being and you have lost your internal frame of reference. You have forgotten that you ever had this inner connection, but you have a vague sense that you have lost something, that something is missing. The fallen beings can use this by creating the belief system that you have fallen into sin, that you were created in sin or that you are in other ways deficient in the eyes of the angry god in the sky. They then offer you a relief from this fear of annihilation by giving you an external frame of reference. If you live up to the requirements of this frame of reference, and if you do so better than other people, you will become acceptable to their god.

You are now trapped in a game of seeking to become better than other people based on some external standard defined by the fallen beings. You may think that by living up to the demands of this standard, you can reach some ultimate achievement here on earth, such as running 100 meters faster than any other human being has ever done. No matter how fast you run on earth, you cannot run your way into heaven. The standards found here on earth are all based on the duality consciousness, the consciousness of anti-christ. As I have attempted to explain in previous books, these standards will *never* give you access to heaven—no matter what any authority on earth says. God is not mocked and God is no respecter of man-made standards.

You now see the illusion. The ego's competition and comparison games all give you the impression that if you are better than other people based on your standard, God will accept you. No matter how much energy you pour into living up to such a standard and no matter how good you become, it does not bring you one step closer to heaven. You are simply feeding your energy into a black hole, and as you know, no matter how much you pour into a black hole, you can never fill it. What the fallen beings have done on earth is to get millions of people to play these competition games, and you can continue to do so indefinitely, or at least until you run out of opportunity.

The realization I wish to pass on here is that you will enter heaven – the ascended state – only by expanding your self-awareness until it can no longer be contained in the material universe. Here then comes a subtle distinction. I said earlier that you can indeed expand your sense of self by going into separation. It might seem as if winning the competition game would expand your sense of self. After all, it might require considerable skill and self-control to be really good at some task. Being better than all other people can certainly expand the ego.

In reality, you do not expand your sense of self by being good at a particular competition game. You expand your sense of self only when you awaken from that game by realizing: "I am more than this separate self that thinks it is better than other separate selves. I am an infinite self and as such it has no value to me to be better than others according to a finite standard." The question is simple: Do you believe it has some special importance to achieve a measurable result here on earth, or do you see any activity as having value only insofar as it expands your consciousness?

Again, you grow in self-awareness only when you awaken from separation. You awaken by realizing: "I am not *that* I am," meaning the separate self you have built. Now, there are two ways to grow in self-awareness. You can build a separate self designed to have certain experiences, and when you awaken from it, you expand your sense of self. You then build another self to have different experiences and this keeps going until you have had enough. This is what we might call the gradual path. The alternative is to build a separate self that you keep adding on to until you have built it to such a level of sophistication that it seems to be superior to any other separate self on earth. Truly, if (note the *if*) you do awaken from that self, then you will have made progress in self-awareness.

The gradual approach was the only approach taken on earth before the fallen beings entered the stage. They are the ones who "invented" the all-or-nothing approach and they did not do this consciously. The fact is that a fallen being will continue building its separate self and if it does awaken from it, it will indeed have had so many experiences that it can very quickly rise to the same level of consciousness as a lifestream that has taken the gradual approach but never entered separation. The big difference being, of course, that it is much more difficult to awaken from a fallen self.

It has indeed happened that fallen beings have awakened. That is why I told the parable about the prodigal son's return. Even a fallen being will be welcomed into the kingdom—once it has fully awakened from separation. The trouble is, however, that many fallen beings simply are not able to awaken, and they end up going to the second death without becoming ascended masters.

How do you awaken from the fallen consciousness? Lifestreams who have entered separation but not the fallen consciousness can be awakened by encountering a spiritual teacher with the Christ consciousness. This teacher gives them a new frame of reference that helps them realize there is something beyond their present state of consciousness, which awakens their desire to have that something. Once you are lost in the fallen consciousness (which is the ultimate degree of separation), you are blinded by the serpentine logic that you can define your own reality. You cannot be awakened by someone teaching you but only by you seeing that your self-created standard simply does not work and does not get you where you want to go.

As I said, a new lifestream that experiments with its co-creative abilities without going into separation will always awaken and expand its sense of self. Once you go into the fallen consciousness, there is no guarantee that you will make it back out. You can indeed create such a "sophisticated" separate self that you become a black hole. You create such a momentum of denial that you can deny anything, and you are the one at the center of the maelstrom of energy. Rather than being in control or being able to use your superior self to get you back out, you are overpowered by your own creation – by your Frankenstein's monster – and you go down with your ship.

I am not trying to awaken the fallen beings. I am trying to awaken those who are not lost in the fallen consciousness to the fact that competition games will never get you to the goal promised by the game. Even athletes who have achieved world championships often end up feeling a sense of emptiness, a sense that "Where do I go now?" The reason is that when you have had enough of playing the competition games on earth, you will want more. Not more *of* the competition but more *than* the competition, more than the separate self can ever offer you. That is when you become the prodigal son who is worthy of a feast with the fatted calf.

Take note that there are two kinds of what scientists call black holes. One is what really is a black hole in the sense that it is created by the fallen beings who suck everything into their downward spiral without ever being filled. The other is a white hole created by an ascended being who is seeking to lift all life up to a higher sense of self. A black hole does become denser and denser and hotter and hotter until the beings trapped in it literally are burning as if in a fiery hell. They are burning because their sense of self has become so narrow that they seem to have no way to escape the internal division that creates the friction that produces the heat. A white hole – in some cases what you call a sun – becomes brighter and brighter in ever-higher vibrations that give you greater and greater freedom and an ever-expanding sense of self.

Spiritual people and competition games

You may think that as a spiritual person you have risen above the competition games. You may have risen above the more obvious competition games, such as being good at sports or having more money or possessions than the Joneses. The fallen beings have created many more subtle competition games, and one of them is the game of thinking that your religion, spiritual teaching or guru is clearly the most sophisticated one on the planet. This is a game played by many religious and spiritual people, even by many ascended master students.

What will bring in The Golden Age of Saint Germain? It is only that a critical mass of people awaken to their spiritual nature and dare to express it. What will bring this about? Not – as many spiritual people think – that millions of people are converted into believing in the right religion, the highest spiritual teaching or the superior guru. What will make a difference is that millions of people are awakened to their inner connection to their I AM Presences, and this can happen through many spiritual teachings even for people who do not follow a spiritual teaching.

We of the ascended masters are seeking to awaken all people who have the potential to be awakened, and for this reason we have given many spiritual teachings. It has never been our goal to convert every human being to be a follower of one teaching. It has been our goal to help every human being transcend its present sense of self until it becomes an open door for the I AM Presence.

What might facilitate the awakening is a universal form of spirituality, but this cannot be defined by one teaching or system. It is something that is floating around in the collective consciousness, and as such it has, of course, been present for decades, gradually growing stronger and being recognized by more people. You can indeed help bring about the spiritual awakening of humankind, but you can do so only when you rise above the competition games defined by the fallen beings in order to fool spiritual people. By being willing to look at your approach to spirituality, you can quickly come to see how you have been influenced by a desire to belong to the ultimate spiritual movement and be recognized by other people, your guru or even the ascended masters as being more sophisticated than other people. When you give up this desire, you will feel an immense freedom.

What is this form of competition a quest for? It is a quest for recognition from an external source. In many cases you see this as other people or the ascended masters and you seek to gain control over us in order to get the recognition that your ego thinks will guarantee your immortality. As long as you seek to control the minds of others, you will never get full control over your own mind.

Furthermore, have I not said that the only thing that will truly satisfy your inner longing is oneness with your I AM Presence? As long as you are seeking recognition from an external source, how can you attain oneness with the Presence that resides in the kingdom that is within you? It simply cannot happen, and you will never feel fulfilled until you awaken and realize it cannot happen, stopping the game of seeking from without what you can only obtain from within.

The most subtle competition game is the one where you think you have to engage in some kind of game in order to get God to give you his kingdom. As long as you believe in the illusion that God is withholding his kingdom from you and that you can – and must – take it through some kind of activity in this world, you will never get it. You will receive God's kingdom only when you stop struggling to get it and recognize the truth in my statement: "It is the father's good pleasure to give you his kingdom."

The fallen beings love it when you think that you have to follow one of their schemes in order to force God to give you what God offers you freely. They love it when you think you have to struggle to get what can only be had through not struggling but simply accepting. When you struggle to control God or win the ultimate competition, the fallen beings are laughing all the way to the bank, the bank where they deposit the energy you are feeding them through your struggle. Instead, follow the Living Christ as I offer you the peace that passeth understanding, the "understanding" created by the fallen consciousness in an attempt to keep you from oneness.

❧

The only problem
with free will is
that most people
have come to believe
it is not truly free.

❧

10 | VALIDATION GAMES

Much of what I have said about competition games can be transferred to validation games. You may have encountered people who walk around in a city mumbling to themselves or perhaps even screaming profanities, obviously being mentally disturbed or even possessed. The ego can be compared to such a person, as it goes through life constantly mumbling: "Validate me, validate me!"

There are many people for whom their entire lives are a quest for validation. They go into a situation subconsciously saying: "Validate me," and when they don't get the validation they seek, they move on to another situation. Of course, they never get the validation they seek because as long as you are asking someone outside yourself to validate you, how could you ever feel validated?

What is the key to feeling validated? Take my saying that unless you become as a little child, you shall not enter the kingdom. The meaning is that you return to the state of innocence with which you were first created. As I have said, you were created without a vision of your I AM Presence but with a sense of connection to it. If you choose to expand that connection – the pearl of great price – you will feel increasingly validated. Or perhaps we can say that validation never becomes an issue for you. Why would you need to be validated when you are constantly feeling the unconditional love from your I AM Presence?

Validation is really a need of the separate self. You start out with a self that is not in complete oneness, but it has a connection to oneness. As long as you continue to expand that connection, you know and experience that you are loved and accepted for who you are. Not in the sense that you are perfect, but in the sense that you are in the process of growing and that you are accepted and loved for who you were created to be. You are loved for who you are, not for what you have or do.

Once you step into the separate self, an entirely new outlook on life is born, and it is what I have called the deficit approach. The separate self senses that it is not good enough for who it is—and it is entirely correct. The separate self cannot take the ultimate consequence of this because it would lead to its own destruction. We might say that the Conscious You does not need to be validated, it simply needs to become conscious of who or what it is. The separate self does feel a need for validation and it can survive only by getting the Conscious You to think that it has to play the validation game by seeking some form of ultimate validation in this world. Of course, the separate self can never come to feel validated so you are on an impossible quest that will continue until you see this and decide to simply walk away from it.

The impossible quest

No matter how much validation you could possible get on earth, it would still leave you feeling empty. This is illustrated by an old fairy tale about a poor fisherman living with his ambitious wife in a mud hut. One day the fisherman catches a large flounder who promises him that if he will let it go, he will be granted three wishes.

When he comes home to his wife, he has to explain why he has no fish for dinner, and after hearing about the wishes, she first wishes that she had a big wonderful house with many servants. To their surprise, the wish is granted. After having lived in this house for a while, the wife begins to feel empty. She then commands her husband to go back to the flounder with her next wish, namely that she be made queen. When the fisherman returns home, he finds a royal castle with his wife on the throne.

The wife has now received the ultimate validation she could possibly achieve on earth. There simply is no way to go higher on earth, yet after a while she again feels that this is not enough. She then commands her husband to go back to the flounder with her third wish, and this time she wants to be God. When the fisherman returns home, he finds his wife sitting in their original mud hut.

This story has often been used by the power elite as a warning that you should know your place in life and not wish for anything more, especially not anything beyond what is defined as human. From a spiritual perspective, it can be interpreted quite differently. The first lesson is that the ego's quest for validation can never be satisfied by anything on earth. No matter the position, riches or honor you might achieve, it will still leave you feeling empty. The ego might then come up with the idea that if you were made God, your emptiness would disappear, and this is indeed what some fallen beings have believed. The separate self can never achieve this, and there will come a point where the separate self will take you into a downward spiral that ends with you creating your own private, inner hell.

Contrary to the story, the Conscious You can indeed become God. This cannot happen by some external force bestowing this honor upon you. It cannot happen as long as you see God as being outside yourself. It can happen only when you begin to follow my call to seek the kingdom of God inside yourself. You can become God by becoming one with your I AM Presence so you can say: "I and my Father are one." At that moment you will have overcome all sense of emptiness and all desire for any kind of earthly honor or validation.

The subtleties of validation

Why does your I AM Presence decide to send an extension of itself into a dense body on a planet like earth? Part of it is that the Presence wants to experience the material world from the inside. The I AM Presence has a desire – deity sires – for experiencing what it is like to look at the world from inside a physical body. The I AM Presence is infinite. It can desire to experience the finite world but its desire is not infinite. There comes a point where the I AM Presence has had enough of a certain experience and desires to move on. The question is whether the Conscious You can move on with the Presence or whether it gets stuck in having a finite experience indefinitely.

The fallen beings have cleverly used the desire to experience the material world in order to cause the Conscious You to become stuck. One way is to create a subtle version of the validation game. This is a topic that very few spiritual people are aware of, yet let me try to explain this.

As I have said, God has given you free will. You have the right to have any experience you want on earth. You even have a right to go into separation and have the experiences you can only have as a separate self. You will, of course, have to pay the price for any experience so that if you misqualify energy you will have to requalify it and bring the material world back to balance. You have the right to have any experience you want until you have had enough of it and want more than the experience.

As I have said, even the I AM Presence has the desire to experience the material world from the inside. The desire of the Presence is finite, meaning that after having a certain experience for a time, it will want to move on. As long as the Conscious You is connected to the I AM Presence, it will also have only a finite desire for any given experience and after some time it will be ready to move on. The fallen beings have no power over the Presence, but they can gain power over the Conscious You if they can trick it into going into separation. The Presence does not desire to experience separation, but the Conscious You can form this desire once it is inside a dense physical body/mind.

The Conscious You can form a desire to experience a certain activity as a separate being, and once it desires to create such a separate self, it can become stuck in another closed loop. The separate self cannot be saturated by having any experience on earth. It is literally like a black hole that will want more of the experience and want to have it in ever-more intense ways. The separate self literally cannot get enough.

Of course, the Conscious You can get enough, but the fallen beings attempt to subvert this by creating a subtle version of the validation game. This game says that you will have had enough only when you have an ultimate experience or reach some kind of ultimate goal.

Take note of the subtle difference. You have a right to have any experience possible on earth. If your desire is pure, your only motivation for engaging in a certain activity is to experience what it is like to be doing this. You enjoy the activity, and once you have enjoyed its various facets to the point where you feel saturated, you simply move on. The validation game adds another dimension. You are now no longer engaging in the activity in order to enjoy the experience but in order to gain some kind of validation by doing the activity. You are seeking to have some kind of ultimate or peak experience. You are seeking for some sense that by doing the activity a certain amount of times, with a certain intensity or better than other people, you feel validated.

What is the problem? What have I just said about validation? It is an impossible quest because as a separate self you can never feel ultimately validated. If you seek ultimate validation through a particular activity, you will never feel saturated by the experience. No matter what you do, the separate self can always imagine something more intense so it will never be enough. Meaning that you will never be able to move on from a particular activity.

For most lifestreams, there is a set of human activities that they have to experience before they feel they have had the full range of human experiences and are ready to begin the spiritual path that leads to the ascension. If you get stuck in one particular activity, how can you ever start the spiritual path?

Human sexuality

There is a difference between doing an act in order to enjoy the experience and then the sense of gaining some kind of validation from having done the experience to a certain degree based on some relative standard. Are you doing it in order to enjoy doing it or in order to enjoy having done it? Let me try to make this less abstract by using sexuality as an example. After all, human sexuality is one among the range of experiences that all lifestreams need to have before they are ready to enter the path to the ascension. It is also one of the more difficult aspects of the human experience to deal with. And yes, I have been in physical embodiment and know how difficult it can be.

Let me first say that we have given teachings that in a distant past, it was not necessary with physical intercourse in order to produce offspring. For a very long time, matter on planet earth has been so dense that the only way to produce new physical bodies was for a man and a woman to have sexual intercourse. It has for a long time been possible for beings to have a desire to experience sex. From a higher perspective, there is nothing wrong or sinful in having a desire to experience sex, as long as it is seen as any other activity you can do with a physical body.

The entire overlay of guilt, shame or sinfulness related to sex was produced by the fallen beings and not in any way by the ascended masters. From our perspective, enjoying sex is the same as enjoying a good meal, building something with your hands or producing a work of art. It is simply one among other human activities that you enjoy until you reach saturation and move on.

Let me now sketch the scenario of a new lifestream that takes embodiment on earth for the first time. In the beginning, it will have to get used to how the physical body works. No matter how well you think you are prepared before you first take embodiment, the density of a physical body will surprise you and will take some getting used to. In the beginning, the new lifestream will typically let the physical body regulate its desire for sex. It might not be too critical about selecting a partner, leaving it up to availability and it might not even enjoy sex, engaging in it as a purely physical activity. There is a physical pressure and it is a matter of relieving it, as you get over hunger by eating. Many human beings on earth are still at that stage.

The next stage is where the lifestream realizes that every activity you can do with a physical body has a psychological component. You can perform an activity in a mechanical way or in such a way that it gives you psychological enjoyment and fulfillment. The lifestream now enters a stage where it becomes focused on having sex for the purpose of producing a certain state of mind. This is, of course, still focused on its own gratification. Although sex, mostly, involves a partner, the person is having sex for the sake of its own enjoyment. Again, many people are still working through this stage.

The next stage is where the lifestream begins to realize that sex really is an activity that involves two people. It now begins to focus more on giving its partner the greatest sense of enjoyment, eventually realizing that only by satisfying your partner do you personally get the greatest enjoyment. This is where a person starts being more discriminative about its sexual partners, often voluntarily limiting the number of sexual partners. This is where people begin to realize that sexual enjoyment can reach a higher level when it is combined with a genuine sense of love for your partner.

The next stage is where a lifestream begins to realize that any physical activity can have a spiritual component. In terms of sex, it is an activity that can help two people experience a sense of oneness with each other, which can be very valuable in terms of helping each of them overcome the identification with their individual selves, even their separate selves. This can then help people realize that sex is not simply a matter of feeling physically attracted and not even of being emotionally attracted. Beyond being in love, there can be a deeper sense of spiritual connection and a sense of having a spiritual purpose for being together. A man and a woman can then engage in sex for the purpose of increasing their sense of spiritual union and even to help each person experience glimpses of union with its I AM Presence.

After having been through this stage, people then realize that even though sex can give you a transcendent experience of oneness with Spirit, the experience is really produced in the mind. You can learn to have that experience without having physical intercourse, and this is the natural next stage on the path. At this point, partners may decide no longer to have sexual intercourse, or they may decide to continue it because it strengthens their sense of unity or because they still enjoy it. When you reach this stage, whether you have sex or not is inconsequential for your spiritual growth.

The impure overlay

What I have outlined here is what we might call the pure scenario, meaning that it is not affected by the fallen consciousness. What the fallen consciousness does is that it creates a dualistic view of sex. Sex is no longer seen as an activity that you do for the pure enjoyment of it; it is given an overlay. In one polarity, sex is seen as wrong, sinful or anti-spiritual. In the other extreme, sex is seen as a way to get validation by having done it a certain amount of times, with as many partners as possible and any number of other comparative measures. You either see sex as wrong and either don't do it or try not to enjoy doing it. Or you see sex as a way to get validation, meaning you also don't enjoy doing it but only enjoy the sense that having done it gives you.

The effect of this scenario is that people get stuck. They get stuck whether they force themselves to abstain from sex or whether they use it to seek validation. What have I just said is the natural or pure scenario? It is that you engage in a human activity and gradually take your enjoyment of it to higher, more refined levels until you have explored all facets of the experience and feel saturated.

Do you see the subtle conclusion? Sex is a natural human desire, a natural human activity. You will not be ready to ascend until you reach the saturation point and feel you are done with sex. If you force yourself to abstain from sex – often because you feel it is dirty or anti-spiritual – how will you ever move through the stages of refining it until you reach saturation?

It is perfectly true that sex can be a very dirty activity, yet this is not an inevitable quality of sex but a consequence of the fallen consciousness. The consciousness of separation perverts everything and drags it down into the mud. Separation always has two opposite polarities. You will *never* escape separation by going into one polarity and seeking to destroy or get away from the other. You will escape separation only by transcending both dualities so you can engage in an activity with a pure and innocent state of mind, until you have enjoyed the activity fully and can truly move on because there is nothing left you want to experience.

Of course, seeking to use sex for validation will also cause you to get stuck. You are now engaging in sex for the sake of having done it. This makes you vulnerable to having sex be the main activity that sucks you into any or all of the various ego games. For example, some people are seeking a sense of power through sex. In the extreme case this can lead to a man becoming a serial rapist or a woman seeking to seduce any man she comes across. It is a pursuit of having the feeling that you can sexually conquer anyone. Of course, sex can also be the entry point into the competition games of seeking to conquer as many people as possible. Or it can lead to the quest for some kind of peak experience where you have sex with the ultimate partner or have it under special circumstances. As I have said, seeking a peak experience will never satisfy you. It will always leave you empty, and your ego will always come up with a new carrot dangling in front of your nose—until the Conscious You awakens and decides that it has had enough of being on the ego's treadmill.

The serpentine logic

I want to add a perspective here. I know well that some fallen beings will take what I have given here and dis-interpret it in various ways. One way is that they will say: "Well, you are saying that God has given us free will and allows us to have any experience we want on earth. What's wrong with having the experience that we want validation or an ultimate experience? We are simply having one of the experiences that are possible on earth so why are you calling us fallen ones and saying we are wrong for doing this?"

My response is that I am not saying there is anything wrong with having this or any other experience possible on earth. Nor am I saying that certain beings (embodied and dis-embodied) should not be doing what they are doing. My role is to represent the universal Christ consciousness to all people on earth. Precisely because of free will, I can only help people when they are open to the Christ consciousness, when they have ears to hear. There are some people on earth who are simply not open to me. I am not in the least concerned with helping such beings. I know that the law of God has set up the School of Hard Knocks so that these people continue to make the knocks harder and harder until they simply can't stand it anymore. Then, when they decide they don't know everything, I can start helping them.

My purpose for giving these teachings is to help those who have not deliberately entered the fallen consciousness but who have been ensnared by it. The law of God gives you the right to try to set yourself up as the almighty ruler of other people. If they allow you to do this and decide to follow you, everyone is simply having the experience they want. The fallen beings have never been content with getting people to follow them

out of a free choice. They have always used the subtleties of
the dualistic mind to deceive people. My role is to simply offer
people the truth that can set them free from the serpentine
deception—if they are willing to leave their nets and follow
me.

The fact is that there are many people on earth who have
already come to the point of wanting to move higher, of wanting to find an alternative to the human struggle. Because they
have been ensnared by the many serpentine lies, they cannot
see how. This is a violation of free will. They want to do better
but they cannot and are trapped. In a higher sense, the fallen
beings have a right to try to deceive people, but they do not
have the right to do this without people having been given an
alternative by a representative of the Christ mind.

In the natural or pure scenario, a lifestream will engage in
a certain activity for the enjoyment of experiencing the activity
itself. As long as you are in this scenario, you are getting the
enjoyment of the experience, and given that you are an infinite
being, you will eventually have had enough of any finite activity. You can never be stuck in a certain activity. You are on a
track, and it is only a matter of time before you feel saturated.

What the fallen beings have done is to create a number of
games that block you from having the actual enjoyment of any
activity. Instead, they seek to get you to strive for a vicarious
experience, a substitute for the real thing. One example is the
validation game where you instead of enjoying sex enjoy having conquered so many different sexual partners. The problem
here is that this is not a real enjoyment because it can never
be filled. You will never have an ultimate sexual experience
because the ego can always define another ultimate experience
that is just beyond your reach.

The natural scenario is that you have actual enjoyment
and that you constantly work towards saturation. In the fallen

scenario, you never have actual enjoyment, you have the promise of an ultimate experience that never comes. When you have one peak experience, they simply move the goal post and you are still unfulfilled. In this scenario you are not on a track towards saturation. You are in a downward spiral that causes you to expend more and more energy – it takes more and more energy to have a more and more intense experience – while still feeling empty, often feeling more and more empty.

In the fallen scenario, you can never be fulfilled. You can awaken only by realizing what is happening, seeing the utter vanity of it and then deciding to simply stop playing the game. It is not a matter of winning the ultimate prize; it is a matter of stopping the game.

In the natural scenario, you get positive experiences until you feel saturated. In the fallen scenario you never gain positive experiences, or you gain them only for a short time. You never feel saturated but always feel like there must be more. There is no way to stop the downward spiral until you see the futility of it and simply walk away. Your ego and the fallen beings will do anything in their power to stop you from walking away from a certain ego game, and their primary tool is the ego dramas, which I will describe in the next book.

You do have a right to have any experience you want for as long as you want. If you feel you want something more than what you have been doing so far, then the way out is to see through the ego games and come to the point where you can stop playing. The real purpose for life on earth is to raise your consciousness. You can raise your consciousness by engaging in sex. This can happen as I described by raising your approach to it and eventually reaching saturation. Each time you step up to a higher approach, you raise your consciousness.

The validation game, or any of the other games, will not raise your consciousness until you abandon it. Again, you have the right to engage in sex in order to seek validation. The long-term question is how easy it is to get out of an activity or approach once you have had enough of it. As I have attempted to explain, the ego games make it so much harder to break free of a pattern even though you have had enough of it.

I champion your right to deny what I am saying here. I already know all the arguments that those in the fallen consciousness will use against my teaching on sex. It is one of their favorite topics, which is why I chose to use it as an example. I champion your right to follow the fallen beings and let them determine your approach to sexuality. When you have had enough of dancing to the tune of the pied piper, come back to me and I will show you how to dance to the tune of your I AM Presence.

There is only one way to get ultimate validation, and that is to be who you are. You already are who you are, you are who God created you to be. The fallen ones want you to think that what God created isn't worthy of validation and you need to live up to a standard they have defined. You need to turn yourself into something different from what God created, something the fallen beings have defined. You will not enter the kingdom until you become as a little child and innocently focus on being who you are without trying to live up to any standard on earth. Only the being who descended from heaven can ascend back to heaven.

11 | RESPONSIBILITY GAMES

The ego will *never* take responsibility for anything. This doesn't mean that people blinded by their egos wont take responsibility for anything. In its never-ending pursuit of seeking to avoid accountability, the ego will indeed seek to make you refuse to take responsibility for anything. If that doesn't work, the ego will gladly seek to make you take responsibility for things for which you are not responsible. It will seek to make you take on more and more responsibility until you think you are responsible for saving the world. This is commonly called a savior complex, and I can tell you from personal experience that you have to overcome it before you can actually become a world savior.

Why the ego cannot take responsibility

Why wont the ego ever take responsibility for anything? Why wont the ego ever stop and say: "It was my fault?" How could it?

I have said that the ego is created out of duality, which always has two opposing polarities. When the Conscious You creates the ego, you do not create one ego, you create two aspects, two spirits. The two original spirits that form the core of your personal ego have since morphed into a multitude of other spirits. Which one of them is responsible for a particular action?

For each action there is not just one spirit involved. The spirits form a hierarchy so for a particular action, there is a line of spirits that all form part of the basis for responding. Which one of them should be held accountable? None of them made the decision and none of them were the sole foundation for the decision so how could any of them be said to be responsible? There are examples of people forming a mob and the group now acts as one entity. How do you single one person out from a mob and say that he or she is solely responsible? Even if you could eliminate all other spirits and get down to the two original ones that form your personal ego, how could one of them be said to be responsible? Why this one and not the other one?

However, when you go to a deeper level, you see that the ego cannot take responsibility because it does not have self-awareness. This is a subtle point that it will be difficult for many students to get, but it is still important to ponder it.

There is an inherent danger in describing the ego. Due to the mechanics of language, it is necessary to name something in order to talk about it. In naming something "the ego" it is easy to give the impression that this is now like a living entity that exists inside your mind, your subconscious mind. When we talk about a spirit, it can sound like we are talking about an entity that is like a person but with no physical body. After all, I do say that the ego is seeking to deceive and manipulate you and that it seeks to stay hidden from you.

Again, we come to a subtle distinction. The ego, even some of the more sophisticated spirits, do indeed have a rudimentary form of consciousness. This does not mean they are like persons. How do we make the distinction? As one example, take animals. An animal in nature has a certain state of consciousness and it is able to observe its environment and respond to stimuli. Scientists normally say that an animal responds based on instinct instead of conscious, reasoned decisions.

Many people will, of course, dispute this because they have pets that they feel have a distinct personality. However, animals that come in close contact with humans are often more sophisticated because they can have an individual nature spirit rather than being part of a group soul. A pet that has been loved by a human and had much contact with that human can become an individualized being that can start he process of expanding its self-awareness. Even a pet will not become individualized in its present incarnation. It will become individualized only as a result of receiving a spirit spark.

As another example, consider the debate about whether it will one day be possible for scientists to build a computer that has the same level of consciousness as a human. There are indeed many people who go through an entire lifetime functioning largely as a computer, meaning every aspect of their lives is determined by the spirits in their subconscious minds. These people never actually make a conscious, reasoned decision. From this perspective, it would be possible to build a computer that could function the same way as many people. What scientists will never be able to do is build a computer that has the higher potential of a human being, namely that of being self-aware. A computer can only act on its programming. It may be able to change its programming in response to its environment, but it will never be able to make a conscious, free choice.

An individual spirit is like an individual computer program. The ego can be compared to the operating system, meaning the overall program that defines the environment or interface of the computer. You may create a program that sorts the emails you receive, throwing some of them away and giving others a special status. If an email gets thrown in the Spam folder, can you say that the program is responsible for doing this? The program simply did what it was programmed to do and had no choice in the matter so how can it be said to be responsible?

Even the ego cannot be said to be responsible because the ego does not make choices—it makes selections. Take note of the difference. You have, over many lifetimes, created an array of spirits that are designed to deal with specific situations. As a general example, say someone blames you for being wrong. You then have a spirit that immediately – and often without you making a conscious choice – starts defending yourself by seeking to refute what the other person is saying. You might also have a spirit that starts attacking the other person, seeking to make him seem wrong in some way that justifies you ignoring what he is saying.

How did these two spirits spring into action? They did so because the ego activated them. The ego did not look at the situation and make a conscious, reasoned choice about how to respond. It simply looked at the situation, determined that it was an attack, and then it selected which spirit or spirits should be activated in order to deal with the situation. The ego did not create the spirits; it simply selected from an array of previously created spirits. You see then that the ego cannot make choices; it can only make selections. Which now makes us realize that responsibility can be assigned only to a being that is capable of making choices rather than selections.

Making choices

As we have said many times, when the student is ready, the teacher appears. Meaning that until the student is ready, the teacher cannot appear. These ego discourses are not meant for everyone because most people are not ready for them. Who are they meant for? They are meant for people who have come to the point where they consciously pursue spiritual growth. What is the end goal of spiritual growth? It is self-mastery, which means that you have followed the call to "have dominion" over the earth.

In Genesis it is said that God created people in his image and likeness and sent them into the world with the command to "multiply and have dominion." This means that you multiply and expand your sense of self until you are able to take dominion over the material realm. What does it mean to have dominion? Many spiritual students think it means to have the power of mind over matter so you can manifest things out of thin air or perform the miracles that I performed. While this may be part of having dominion, the core is that you have complete control over your own mind so you can choose your response to any situation rather than letting the situation determine your reaction and response.

What have I said previously? The entire purpose for the material universe is to serve as an educational device to help self-aware beings grow in consciousness. How does the material world do this? It does so by presenting you with a very complex environment, and because you are in a physical body, you will have to respond to that environment in some way. The question now becomes how you respond. Your response will be determined exclusively by your reaction to any given situation. Do you make a free choice or do you let the ego select from an array of predefined spirits whose responses can be predicted?

Let us make a distinction between your response, which is the physical action you take, and your reaction, which is how you experience the situation inside your own mind (what you think and feel about it). The court systems of the world will say that you are responsible for your actions. This is correct, but how do you take control over your actions? Only by taking control over your *re*-actions. How do you take control over your reactions? By making choices instead of selections.

Say you encounter a situation where you are walking down the street at night and someone comes running towards you with an instrument in his hand that is glittering as if it was made of metal. Do you perceive this as a threat, go into fear and either flee or seek to fight what you see as an attacker? Or can you – in a split second – step outside the situation and respond from a higher perspective? Can you respond with love rather than fear? Can you make a creative decision rather than responding with fight or flight? You now see that the common concept of fight or flight describes the polarity of two opposing spirits. Yet the principle applies to every aspect of human psychology.

Most people spend their entire lives responding to situations that life throws at them. They respond by selecting from an array of predefined options. These options are a mixture of what has been defined for them as they were growing up and what they carry with them from past lives. People have in past lives created a large number of spirits and during their upbringing they either reinforced these spirits or created new spirits. In every situation they encounter, they react by letting their egos select which spirit is going to handle the situation. Their actions simply follow from the spirit's reaction to the situation. They are not making a conscious, reasoned or creative choice but simply allowing their response to be determined by predefined spirits.

Now, I am not blaming people for this. When a new lifestream first takes embodiment in an environment as complex as earth, you will not have the self-awareness necessary to make conscious, creative choices. As I said in the first book, it is virtually inevitable that new lifestreams create an ego and an array of spirits. As a lifestream matures and begins to reach for self-mastery, it is absolutely necessary that you claim your ability to stop making selections and to start making real choices. Which part of you can do this? The ego will never be able to do so. Only the Conscious You can do this.

Understanding the Conscious You

Why is the Conscious You able to make choices rather than selections? Because the Conscious You is created as what I have called pure awareness, meaning the Conscious You has no individuality. This means that the Conscious You is not what you normally call a person that has a personality or individuality.

Again, the mechanics of language will make this sound like a contradiction. I have said that the Conscious You is an individualized extension of the Creator's being and of your I AM Presence. I am also saying that the Conscious You has no individuality. How can you deal with this seeming contradiction?

You cannot deal with it through the human intellect; you can deal with it only by actually experiencing yourself as pure awareness. Perhaps you have had this experience, perhaps not. If not, I encourage you to use the tools we have given in order to purify your consciousness to the point where it will happen naturally. [See *www.transcendencetoolbox.com*.]

If you have had some glimpse of pure awareness, you will know that it is possible for you to be aware without being aware of anything. You are conscious, but you have no thoughts and no sense impressions. This experience can take two basic forms. You can experience yourself as a point or you can experience yourself as being everywhere. The common thread is that you experience an awareness that is beyond the material universe, as the material world is by definition finite. That which is finite is neither a single point nor omnipresence. Because the Conscious You has no individuality, it is not a finite but an infinite being. The Conscious You can step into a finite identity and forget it is an infinite being, but it can never lose its ability to step outside the finite identity and once again experience its own infinity.

You may have heard scientists say that before the Big Bang all matter and energy was compressed into a singularity. Unfortunately, scientists find it difficult to describe what a singularity is. What they *can* say is that it is like a single point that has no extension in space. This gives us an important clue because if a point has no extension in space, it means there can be no division within it. There is no extension in space so there is no room to create a division into two or more separate parts.

This is how the Conscious You starts its existence. It is a singularity. It exists as a point-like self, a sense that is aware that: "I am here." It does not have the sense "I am this" or "I am that." It has a sense that "I am" and it has a sense of being a single point. The task of the Conscious You is to expand its self-awareness until it reaches a state of experiencing: "I am everywhere in the consciousness of my Creator." In order to go from here to there – in order to go from one form of infinity to another form of infinity – the Conscious You must go through the finite world.

In the finite world, everything has an extension in space. This means that there is room for a division within it, which makes it possible that it can have characteristics that set "this thing" apart from any other thing. The Conscious You takes embodiment by creating a self that has extension in space and has what seems like an individuality. The Conscious You is creating a self through which it can express itself in the material world.

The task of the Conscious You at this point is to gradually create a wider and wider sense of self. In the ideal scenario, it is possible for the Conscious You to create this self without losing its awareness that it is still a point-like being. It knows that it has created a self and stepped into it but that it has not become that self. It is more than its self. As the Conscious You creates many different and gradually more sophisticated selves, it begins to realize that it is more than any self that it could possibly create in the material world, and this is when it can begin the process of Christhood leading to the ascension.

This is also when the Conscious You begins to experience infinity as omnipresence instead of a singularity. The ascension is a process where you move beyond seeing yourself as a point and beyond seeing yourself as a self with extension in space to seeing yourself as an omnipresent self. As a newly ascended master you will have a sense of omnipresence but not the fullness of it. You then start gradually intensifying the omnipresence until you reach the ultimate stage, namely the Creator consciousness.

As I have said, going into separation and the fallen consciousness is not necessary in order to complete the process of growth in self-awareness. It is a possible stage towards that growth, and once you awaken from it, you will indeed have grown.

What happens when you go into separation is that you forget your point-like sense of self and come to experience that you are a self with an extension in space. You are defined by individual characteristics and your survival depends on them. In order to secure that survival, it seems there is only one way, namely to take your individual characteristics as far as they can be taken in space. You must take them so far that they can control any circumstance that you could encounter in the material world.

Choice versus selection

Let me try to illustrate this with a linear (thus not entirely adequate) image. The material world is finite, meaning that although you can choose to create many different selves, there is a limit to what can be created (at least on this one planet). Let us say that in the very beginning, the Conscious You is standing in the center of a circle. As you know, the circle is a symbol for infinity because it seemingly has no beginning and no end. We can turn the circle into a symbol for the material world by dividing it into a circumference with 360 degrees or angles.

Imagine that you are standing in a single point that is the center of a circle. The circle has 360 degrees on the circumference, which means you can draw a pie-like figure where each degree forms a triangular shape. You are the Conscious You in its singular or centered stage. You can choose to go into any of the 360 different kinds of selves available in your circle in order to experience what it is like to look at the material world through that self.

Now imagine that you pick one self and the triangular shape can be compared to a road where your perspective becomes wider as you walk down it. As you react to the larger world through this particular self, you expand that self and in a sense this expands your awareness. You become more aware of what the world is like, but this happens only within the boundaries defined by this self. The farther you walk away from the center, the more you expand your perspective so it seems like a good thing to walk away from the center—and this is indeed what you are meant to do. You are meant to expand your awareness of the world as an intermediate step towards expanding your self-awareness.

One day you reach the circumference of the circle, and now you simply cannot expand your perspective on the world any more through this particular self. How do you grow in consciousness from this level? If you have not entered separation, you still know that you are a point-like self in the center of the circle. You can easily turn around and look towards the center, you can instantly abandon the self you have created (letting it die or giving up this life in order to return to the center). You do this by saying: "I have not become this self, I am more than this self." Once back in the center, you can choose another self and repeat the process. Once you have gone around the circle and experienced life in the material world from all 360 angles (in reality many more are possible), you can come to the conclusion: "I am more than any self in this world," meaning you are ready to enter the process of ascending to a higher world. Your causal body will contain the experiences of seeing the world from all these different perspectives and you will have many nuances in your causal body.

Separation and the use of force

If you go into separation, you likewise pick a specific self and you go towards the outer boundary of that self, that slice of the pie. In separation, you have forgotten your center, and you cannot turn towards the center, let alone return to it. You do experience that you have reached the outer limits for how far you can go with that self, but you are not able to see that you can return to center and pick another self. You still have the drive to expand your consciousness, but now your only option is to think that you can do this only by expanding this one self.

How can you expand the one self when you have reached the circumference of the circle? You can do so by breaking down the separation between your slice of the pie and the one next to it. Your separate self takes over the territory of what it sees as another separate self and overpowers it. This requires you to fight all of the people who have also come to the outer limits of their slice of the pie, and it requires you to subdue all the ones who are not yet as extreme as you are. This inevitably makes your life a perpetual struggle.

Take note of the distinction. In the first scenario, you start by getting to experience everything within one slice of the pie. You then experience everything within another slice of the pie, meaning you have a more nuanced experience. We can say that you color the first slice with one color, then move on and color the next slice with another color. Eventually you have gone around the circle and colored every slice with a different color, experiencing all of the different colors available on earth. You have now had the fullness of experiences that the learning environment of earth has to offer.

In the second scenario you also color the first slice with a particular color. In seeking to break down the barrier to the next slice, you color that slice with the same color as the first, only it becomes a shade more intense and slightly altered by the other color. You can also go around the circle this way, coloring each slice with a more intense shade until you have filled in the entire circle. You will then also have reached the limits for what you can experience on earth and you will feel that this planet is restricting you.

In the first scenario, you have experienced the fullness of the color palette available on earth so you are now able to choose to ascend to a world that has even more colors than on earth. In the second scenario, you have experienced earth only through the shades of one color. Your only option is to descend into a world that has different shadings of that color than what is found on earth, meaning a world with a more limited color palette. It is possible that after having gone around the circle of earth (or even before), you can awaken from separation and remember your center. You can then also transcend the earth by giving up the separate self. You will still not have experienced the full color palette of earth, which means you might want to go back or at least fill in the holes from the ascended realm.

If you do not awaken, you will descend to a world that is more limited than earth, and this can continue until your options are reduced to just one that simply becomes more and more intense until you can no longer stand it and cry out for deliverance. Deliverance will be offered to you, but deliverance can be delivered only through your own choices.

Choice and selection revisited

This returns us to the topic of choice versus selection. When you have not forgotten your center, you have a real choice. You can become aware that you have had enough of seeing the world through a particular self. You can return to the center, and now you can make a choice between each of the remaining slices of the pie. In the center, any option is open to you and you are free to choose.

When you are in separation, you reach the circumference of the circle, but you are not aware of the choice to return to center. You are not actually seeing that you are limited by your self. Instead, you think you are limited by the two selves, the two slices of the pie, on each side of your slice. You start fighting them, seeking to subdue them through force, forcing your color upon them and the people who have chosen those kinds of selves. Once you conquer those two slices, you will feel limited by the two next ones, and so on until you have conquered the whole circle.

Where does this process take place? It takes place entirely within your own mind. You are not actually conquering the world. You are simply eliminating all different colors from your field of view. Instead of seeing the circle as having 360 degrees that are all equally valid, you see one color as the only right one and you seek to force that color to overlay and block out all the other options. You may be successful in making a lot of other people agree with you and engage in the process of blocking out a certain slice of the pie from the collective consciousness. Theoretically, it could happen that the inhabitants of an entire planet blocked out all other options but one. As soon as that would happen, the planet would self-destruct.

Elevating one option to the status of superiority takes away your ability to make real choices. When you encounter other people with a different perspective on life, you no longer have the option of saying: "Hey, these people seem to have an interesting life experience, I wonder what that would be like? Could it possibly enrich my own life experience?" The greater purpose of having people with many different perspectives on the same planet is that it makes it harder for everyone to believe that there is only one right way to experience life, and this reduces the risk that the inhabitants will go into the separate scenario. It gives everyone the chance to see that there are many different perspectives and that knowing more than one enriches your life experience.

When you are in separation, you will see the other people as a threat, and you will not be able to make the creative choice: "Hey, I would like to experience that perspective also." Instead, you will only see a selection of options for how you can defend yourself from the threatening perspective and perhaps even destroy that perspective and the people who are in it. These many options have been cleverly created by the fallen beings after they came to this planet, and I will talk more about them in the next book.

When you have forgotten your center, you can see only the options created through the mind of anti-christ. You may select one of these, but this is not making a real choice. A creative choice can only be made from the center of the Christ consciousness, which sees oneness beyond diversity.

What exactly is your responsibility?

Having set a fruitful foundation, let us now return to the topic of responsibility. You have a dual responsibility on this planet. First, you are responsible for experiencing the world and responding to it. You do this by making a free choice to enter one slice of the pie and experience the world through it. Your other responsibility is to retain a connection to your center so you never forget that you are an infinite being experiencing the finite world and not a finite being who is a product of the finite world.

Although the courts of the world will say you are responsible for your actions, you are first and foremost responsible for your state of mind. We might say that you are responsible for making choices in such a way that one choice does not take away your freedom to make other choices. You are responsible for retaining your ability to make creative choices, choices that are centered in the oneness of the Christ consciousness.

As I have said, on a planet as dense as earth, it is almost inevitable that you lose the Christ awareness and become blinded by separation. There is no reason to blame yourself for this. This also means that when you discover the spiritual path and consciously decide that you want to walk it, you need to recognize that your primary responsibility is to reclaim your ability to make free choices. That means you must acquire the ability to discern based on the Christ consciousness. This is the only way you can reclaim your ability to make conscious choices, rather than making the unconscious selections between different spirits.

You are indeed an individualized being. You have a point-like sense of self and it is this self that can make choices. All true choices are made from the undivided center. You have created a self that has an extension in space, yet this self does not make choices; it simply makes selections. It cannot define the options; it can only select from predefined options.

Your primary responsibility is to take command over your own mind, your own state of mind. The spiritual path is *not* a process of spiritualizing or perfecting the separate self. It is a process of gradually dismantling it, letting it die, until you have lost your life in order to follow Christ to the center of being.

Take note of the important conclusion. You are an individualized being. You are responsible for your individual lifestream and *nothing* else on this planet. You are responsible for making free, conscious choices from the center of *your* being. You are not responsible for the choices made by any other being on this planet or anywhere else in the material universe. You are responsible for making your own choices and not for making choices for other beings. That is *their* responsibility. As self-awareness is point-like, responsibility is likewise point-like.

Why people do not take responsibility

We can now see why people fail to take responsibility for their situation. When you see life through the filter of the ego and a number of spirits, you cannot take responsibility. The arrow of responsibility – in order to be effective – must point towards a single point. "YES! I am responsible." If you see yourself as a diffuse or divided being (a being that has an extension in space) where exactly should responsibility be placed? The ego and the spirits have so many divisions that there is never a single point where to place responsibility and thus people refuse to take responsibility.

This is, of course, a difficult proposition. It is deeply ingrained in the collective psyche that there are causes and there are effects. When you take an action with your physical body, it will have an effect and you – as a body – will be said to be responsible for that effect. If you – as a psychological being – do not have a center, how can you accept that you are responsible? You very easily get sucked into the myriad games invented by the ego and the fallen beings, of deflecting responsibility.

From this has been created an almost innumerable amount of spirits that are programmed to deflect responsibility away from yourself. Every effect must have a cause, and if the cause is not you, then the cause must be somewhere else—meaning it must be someone else. If you are not responsible, someone else must be.

As a spiritual seeker, you will already have overcome some of this tendency to deflect responsibility away from yourself. You have learned to take some responsibility for your actions and you have learned to discipline your actions. As a sincere spiritual seeker there are some actions you would never even consider taking because they simply do not fit with your self-image. The same, of course, holds true for many other people on earth, some being religious and some not being outwardly spiritual.

The more subtle, and for a spiritual seeker more dangerous, responsibility games do not have to do with your actions. Instead, these games are centered around beliefs and attitudes to life.

To be or not to be responsible

Again, let us look at the court systems of the modern, demo-
cratic world. It is a principle of democracy that people have as
much freedom as possible, including the freedom of speech.
In order for you to have freedom of speech, you must have
freedom to think. What you do not have in a democracy is
freedom of action. A democracy sets rules for how people live
together, meaning no individual has a right to take actions that
harm other individuals. A democracy is – ideally – reluctant to
get into people's heads and tell them what to think and how
to approach life. It is generally held that you can think and
feel whatever you like as long as you are able to refrain from
actions that harm others.

What this points to is exactly what I have said above,
namely that you are an individual being and your primary
responsibility is your own state of mind. It is also held by the
court systems that you are – generally – not responsible for the
actions or the state of mind of other individuals. This is where
we need to make another subtle distinction.

When you live together with other people – as a couple, a
family, a village or an entire planet – each individual contrib-
utes to the overall environment. As we have explained, the
environment on earth has four levels, namely identity, mental,
emotional and physical. The environment in which you live is
largely produced by what each individual has put into it, accumulated over time. From this perspective, other people's sense
of identity, their thoughts and feelings do have a direct impact
on the environment in which you live. It is very tempting to
adopt the attitude that the only way to improve your living
environment is to change the minds of other people. This
can then lead people into an innumerable amount of games

designed to make you feel responsible for changing the state of mind of other people.

There are many people who feel it is vitally important – even of epic importance – to convert other people to their particular religion. There are people who feel it is vitally important to get people to abandon all religion. There are people who feel it is vitally important to convert other people to their political persuasion. There are people who direct all of their energies and attention towards changing the minds of other people in other ways, even by using the teachings given by the ascended masters.

Now let me build on what I have given earlier and cut to the chase. Only the "man" who descended from heaven can ascend back to heaven. You entered the material world as a point-like being and you will exit it *only* as a point-like being. Your ascension is an individual event. It does *not* in any way, shape or form depend on the choices made by any other individual being. It depends exclusively on your choices, and your choices depend exclusively on your state of mind.

I know very well that there is what seems like a contradiction here. Many people on this planet are completely consumed by their own self-interest. They do not consider what consequences their lifestyle has for other people or the environment, let alone for the collective consciousness. As you begin to awaken from this selfishness and become open to the spiritual path, you will go through a phase where you take more and more responsibility: "No, I can't do this because it destroys the environment. No, I can't buy this because it was made in a sweatshop. No, I can't do this because it produces negative energy." As you become increasingly aware that even your state of mind has an effect on the total environment on earth, you begin to accept more and more responsibility.

You also become increasingly aware of how interconnected everything is and you become aware of many problems and threats that the more selfish people never consider. It is very easy to reason that as you are changing your state of mind, the only way to solve some of the major problems you now see on earth is that other people do the same. This is where many well-meaning spiritual people get sucked into the more subtle responsibility games.

Again, I will talk more about this in the next book, but for now let me give you something to ponder. The earth is a very complex learning environment whereby I mean that it is designed to accommodate a broad range of students. This is not hard to see when you consider the range of people's level of consciousness. I earlier said there are 360 slices of the pie, but then there are people who have gone into separation and used any of those degrees to create a separate self.

Let us now make a clear distinction between the ideal scenario and the current situation. As you raise your spiritual awareness, you begin to have an intuitive sense of how planet earth could be according to its highest potential. You also become more aware of how far away it currently is. The crucial distinction you need to make here is that planet earth is not currently meant to outpicture its highest potential. It is meant to be a kind of half-way house for lifestreams who are beginning to move out of separation but have not yet done so.

You then need to realize that people can move out of separation only through their own choices. Before they can make a real choice to move back towards the center, they often need to go all the way to the extreme boundaries of a particular slice of the pie. They even sometimes need to break down the barriers between the slices and seek to conquer the earth through one sense of self. This is currently allowed on earth and it is indeed within the overall plan of the ascended masters that the earth functions in this capacity. God has given all beings free will. Earth is currently a holding place for many beings who have used their free will to go into separation. It is allowed that they outplay their separate selves until they have taken them so far to the extreme that they can no longer stand themselves, making a real choice to change. You have gone through the exact same process and you have done so in your own way and according to your own time schedule. Does it not stand to reason that you have an obligation to let other people do the same?

Be an example

If you do not like current conditions on earth, you have two options. One is that you can focus all of your attention on making your ascension so you can get out of here. If you are to ever make your ascension, you will do so only as an individual being. This means you must take full responsibility for yourself and abandon all sense of responsibility for others. It may seem like making your ascension is the ultimate form of selfishness, and in a sense it is. As I said: "And I, if I be lifted up from the earth, will draw all men unto me." When you make your ascension, you create such a powerful momentum that it lifts the consciousness of the entire planet and this is an invaluable contribution to raising the whole. Take note that it is done by changing your own mind and giving up all attempts to change the minds of other people.

As a sincere spiritual seeker, you are constantly working towards the point where you can qualify for your ascension. Can't you do something in the meantime that will also help raise the whole? You are in a sense doing something by raising your consciousness. What you can also do is to be an example of how a person with a higher level of consciousness deals with the intricacies of everyday life in its current form. You see the difference? Many spiritual seekers almost refuse to engage in everyday life because they see it as not spiritual. It is possible to see every aspect of life as spiritual and to give an example of how you can deal with everyday life from a more spiritual form of awareness.

The difference is fundamental. Many spiritual people have been sucked into the games of seeking to influence other people's state of mind and get them to make more spiritual choices. This is a direct violation of the Law of Free Will, which is the most important law for the material universe. The alternative is to become a living example and demonstrate that a more spiritual awareness can lead to a richer everyday life. Thereby, you will show people that there is an alternative to separation and this will inspire some people to change their minds through making creative choices.

Let me make a clear statement. Any time – *any time*– you seek to directly influence other people's state of mind, you are acting from the ego and you are sucked into one of the games created by the fallen beings. You will not – *not ever* – change this planet by seeking to change the minds and choices of other people. You will do so *only* by changing your own mind. Remember my call to let your light shine before men so they can see that this light is not coming from the material world. It is coming from the spiritual world because you have chosen to become an open door for the infinite in the finite world. By seeing that you have done so, some will realize that what one has done, all can do. This is all *you* can do and should try to do on this planet.

Accept what is your personal responsibility and abandon all sense of responsibility for others.

12 | BLAME GAMES

My discourse on responsibility games is not complete in itself. As I said, the ego will never accept responsibility but it will gladly seek to get *you* to accept responsibility for what is not your responsibility. This can be other people, as just explained, or it can be responsibility for the ego's selection of the response to a given situation or life in general. The ego always has a division into at least two, meaning there is one spirit that denies all responsibility for a particular situation and its outcome and there is another spirit that projects at you that you are to blame.

Take a minute to think about this. In any situation you encounter in life, there will be at least two spirits. When you face the situation or its outcome, there is one spirits that projects that you are not responsible and another that projects that you are to blame. Obviously, these two spirits are completely opposite, which means that it is difficult to listen to them both at the same time. Doing so leads to stress, which is what psychologists call "cognitive dissonance." You are seeking to hold two mutually exclusive views at the same time. For most people, one of these spirits will be dominant. Which one will it be for you? That depends on which of the two seems the most real to you given the situation and your present level of spiritual maturity. Basically, if the one spirit fails to convince you that you are not responsible, you will be open to the one that says you are to blame.

At the lower end of the scale of maturity, you have people who are completely selfish, and they will listen to the spirit that says they are not responsible. As you begin to awaken to the spiritual path, it is inevitable that you will accept more personal responsibility, and this will make you vulnerable to the spirit that blames you. You can make the path so much easier for yourself by realizing that as a spiritual seeker, you will have to go through a schizophrenic phase where you alternate from one spirit to the other until you can finally begin to dismiss both spirits. It is not a matter of determining which spirit is right; it is a matter of seeing that they are both unreal.

How spirits are created

Let me now give you a more nuanced picture. I have said that before any fallen beings were allowed to embody on earth, the original inhabitants had started to go into separation. This means they had started to create a number of spirits based on separation but not on the fallen consciousness. The spirits were originally created by individuals and existed only in the energy fields of individuals. Over time, so much energy and consciousness had been projected into these spirits that they began to have an existence in the collective consciousness.

Collective spirits exist at one of the three other levels, namely identity, mental and emotional. The importance is that once collective spirits were created, it now became easier for people in embodiment to go into separation. People could open up their emotional body, for example, to a collective spirit without realizing what they were doing. Once a spirit invaded their individual energy field, it could quickly overpower their emotions. When fallen beings were allowed to enter the energy field of earth, they came in at all four levels. Some of them then started intensifying and perverting the collective spirits in the three higher levels while at the same time creating new spirits based on the fallen consciousness. This now formed a very subtle cocktail and it caused many people to drink the Cool Aid.

The fallen beings who embodied physically would have the lowest level of self-awareness, meaning they were – although they seemed sophisticated compared to many other people – marionettes that were controlled by fallen beings in the higher levels. As I have explained, Hitler or Stalin may have seemed powerful, but they were almost entirely controlled by fallen beings in the higher levels.

The physical fallen beings were used to force people into a simple action-reaction trap. The fallen beings would physically violate the free will of other people, for example through overt force. It was inevitable that some people would respond to this through force and then other fallen beings would now blame people for responding. One group of fallen beings would provoke a response and another group of fallen beings would blame people for their response to the first group.

The result was that people would now go into a dualistic reaction to the blame, and they would either seek to deflect the blame by denying responsibility (or attacking the accuser) or they would accept the blame and seek to compensate for what they had done. What happened at the higher levels was that people unconsciously opened their energy fields to the spirits created by the fallen beings. There were spirits at the emotional, mental and identity levels and some people opened themselves up to one, others to several such spirits. The spirits would now invade people's personal energy fields and often overpower them.

The effect was that people would feel that they were facing a situation that seemed unbearable, and in order to get relief from this, people would then create individual spirits to deal with the collective spirits. This led people into a never-ending game where they responded to the violations of the fallen beings through spirits created by the fallen beings and then created more and more spirits. The net effect being that the more spirits you have in your energy field, the more your attention is directed outwards and the more difficult it becomes for you to reconnect to your center. How can you ever rediscover the stillness of your center when your mind is a battlefield with numerous spirits constantly screaming for your attention?

How do you get off this treadmill? We have given many tools for invoking spiritual assistance. For example, you can invoke the protection of Archangel Michael so spirits cannot as easily gain entry into your energy field. You can call to Elohim Astrea to cut you free from collective spirits and to bind and consume individual spirits. You can use the invocations given by the Maha Chohan to set yourself free from spirits [See the *Flowing With the River of Life Workbook*.]

The most important way to start gaining back some peace of mind is to raise your awareness and start taking command over your own mind and energy field. We of the ascended masters have given many teachings and tools for doing this but people can also do it through careful self-observation. You can use the two main abilities of the Conscious You, namely the ability to step outside your current sense of self and experience infinity and the ability to look at yourself and ask: "Why do I keep doing this when I don't like the results?"

The bottom line is that free will is the most important law so no spirit can gain entry into your energy field unless you invite them. The fallen beings have, as I described, created many subtle schemes for getting you to open yourself up to

spirits without knowing what is happening. You can counteract all of them by becoming aware and by deciding that you
will no longer engage in these patterns of behavior, feelings,
thoughts or sense of identity. My purpose for giving these ego
discourses is to help you raise your awareness, look in the mirror, see the tricks your own ego is using and then decide: "This
simply is not a reflection of who I am."

How to stop blaming others

As I have said, the most important step you can take towards
taking control of your own mind is to decide that you will completely and utterly stop seeking to change the minds of other
people. This means (among other things) that you will stop
using the blame game, which is simply a way to control you
and others, a way that springs from the fallen consciousness.

Let me say that in another way. Any time – *any time* – you
engage in blaming yourself or other people, you are opening
yourself up to the control of impure spirits and through them
to control from the fallen beings. Everything in the material
world is energy, meaning every thought or feeling carries a certain vibration. Blame is a vibration that simply does not exist
in the spiritual realm. The Christ mind contains no traces of
blame whatsoever. It is only in the mind of anti-christ that
blame can exist.

Why do I say this? The core of our teaching about the
Conscious You is that it is pure awareness, which means that
it cannot be changed by anything it encounters in the material realm. This means something extremely important. You
may create many types of separate selves and you may enter
into them and commit the most incredible physical atrocities.
No matter what you might have done, the Conscious You has
not been changed by it. That is why you can never lose the

potential to "become as little children" and enter the kingdom of God within you.

How can people commit unspeakable atrocities? Because they have forgotten that they are pure awareness and have come to identify themselves as a self created from separation. This is exactly what the fallen beings want, and their goal is that once people on earth have entered separation (which is not difficult to attain) they will never get out of it. To this end, the fallen beings have created an elaborate web of blame games that have the primary purpose of making you believe that if you have done something bad, then you have become a bad person. In reality, you are who you are. It is only in separation that you will think you are who you think you are. You can – at any time – awaken from this illusion and connect to reality through the Christ mind—this is my body which is broken for you.

Here is the simple equation. Every time you blame someone else for being a bad person or having made a mistake, you are opening yourself up to the blame energy created by the fallen beings. You are literally making yourself an extension of the fallen beings, and there is no faster way to make karma. You are also creating a spirit that simply lives to blame others, perhaps even one that takes pleasure in blaming others. Each time you allow blaming energy to flow through you, you solidify and intensify that spirit, which means it will have more and more power over you, making it harder for yourself to escape.

There is a subtle mechanism embodied in the statement: "Vengeance is mine, saith the Lord, I will repay." The deeper meaning is that God has set up a law that returns to you any energy you send out. It may not happen in this lifetime, but it will happen. When someone else does something that violates you or others, you have no need to seek to blame or punish that person. The laws of God will take care of this unfailingly, and I can assure you that God's law does not need the assistance of human beings. What the fallen beings have done is create a set of subtle blame and punishment games based on the underlying illusion that the Creator is not capable of taking care of its own creation. Human beings must step in and correct the errors and punish the perpetrators that God's law cannot take care of. This is all one giant illusion and it only seeks to keep you trapped in the consciousness of anti-christ.

You cannot create one spirit that blames others. You must create a pair, one that directs blame outwards and one that directs it inwards. Surely, you can spend a long time being consciously focused on the one that blames others, but you still cannot escape the subconscious influence of the one that seeks to blame *you*. The effect being that you must engage in an elaborate set of rules and behaviors designed to demonstrate that you are not doing something wrong and you are not to blame. If the games that seek to blame people are unreal, what do you think is the case for the games that are designed to help you escape blame? If all of your attention and energy is engaged in unreal activities, what are your chances of returning to reality? Where your treasure – meaning what you put your conscious attention upon – is, there will your heart and mind be also.

Quite frankly, there is no ascended master who can directly work with a student who is still trapped in the blame game. There are indeed many students who have used ascended master teachings to create or reinforce blame games. I am not saying such students cannot benefit from our teachings, but we cannot engage in a direct student-teacher relationship with a student until he or she stops blaming others and starts focusing on changing his or her own mind. It simply isn't possible, for the student will not be able to follow our directions and will make karma for rejecting what we offer. We can only offer such people an outer teaching.

Escaping the blame game

How do you escape the blame games? By being willing to take an honest look at yourself and consider whether you are engaged in these games. To this end, let me give you one measure that you can apply.

The most subtle effect of the blame games is that they put you in a state of constant tension, of being on edge. This means you tend to take everything that happens to you personally. You react in any number of ways that demonstrate you are in tension. The more you tend to take things personally, the more you are trapped in blame games. How can you escape them? By realizing that nothing on earth is personal and thus you should not take anything personally.

I have given you two pieces of information that can help you free yourself from all blame games. One is that the Conscious You is pure awareness and has not been changed by anything you have done or experienced on earth. The other is that free will is individual and is the most important law of the universe. When you put these two together, you see several conclusions:

• Nothing anybody does to you can change you in any way. Why feel threatened by anything in this world?

• Others may cause you to choose to create a spirit in order to react to them, but you must choose to create it, which means you can also choose to uncreate it.

• All people act and talk based on their current level of consciousness, meaning the amount of spirits they have in their consciousness.

• Most people have so many spirits that very little they do or say is deliberate or conscious. People's actions and words come from their subconscious spirits.

• A spirit is not deliberately and consciously attacking you, any more than your computer is seeking to offend you personally. The spirit is simply mechanically acting on its programming. Why take personal what is not personal?

• Sure, another person may attack you very deliberately and personally. That person is simply taken over by his or her blaming spirits, and if it wasn't you, the spirits would find another target. Why take this personally and feel you have to respond?

• You are also reacting to life based on your current state of consciousness, including the spirits you have in your subconscious mind. Both your ego and several spirits will seem to take everything personally. Does that mean *you* have to take everything personally? After all, the ego is not self-aware and cannot truly take anything personally—it simply acts on its programming and appears to be taking things personally.

• Take note of what I said. The ego is created to take things personally so *you* don't have to. This will not work, as you still experience life through the perception filter of the ego. The ego doesn't actually feel bad; *you* feel bad and that is why you need to leave the ego behind.

- You have self-awareness. You have chosen to take things personally—and you can at any time choose to un-choose that choice.

Pondering these facts can help you to stop taking it personally when life or other people do something to you. But what about when you think that you have made a mistake and start blaming yourself?

Stop blaming yourself

Again, blame does not come from the Christ mind. Truly, the Conscious You is not blaming itself—it is a spirit that is blaming the Conscious You. Again, this is simply what the spirit was programmed to do by the fallen beings so why take this personally?

Yes, you did create the spirit or – in the case of all blaming spirits – you accepted it into your energy field. But what you have let in through choice, you can also expel through choice—when you take responsibility for the fact that you were the one making that choice.

Now comes another subtlety. I have said that in order to manifest Christhood, you need to take full responsibility for your life. Does that mean you have to take responsibility for everything you do or say? Not so, because much of what you do or say is not the result of a conscious choice made by the Conscious You, it is the result of a selection made by the ego to activate a certain spirit that then responds according to its programming.

Do you see what the ego and the fallen beings are trying to do? They are trying to get you to react to their attacks through one spirit. Then another spirit blames you for the action. You are now trapped in having to react to your own internal reaction to your action. Often you then go into trying to either defend what you did or to feel guilty about it and compensate for it. What is the result? You – the Conscious You – are now trapped in reacting to an action taken by a spirit. You are focused on the action, and you think that *you* took that action. Meaning you are now focused on stopping yourself from taking similar actions in the future or compensating for the actions you have taken. You are focused on changing the consequences of an action, not on changing your state of consciousness. The net result is that the spirit who took the action remains hidden, as does the ego that selected the spirit.

I have told you to take responsibility for yourself. I am now telling you to stop taking responsibility for actions taken by the spirits in your subconscious mind. Seems contradictory? Then step back and look at the greater perspective. My concern as a spiritual teacher is to free you from any pattern of action-re-action that keeps you trapped in the mind of anti-christ. Any action taken by a spirit comes from the mind of anti-christ and as such it has no reality or consequence for your growth in self-awareness.

Take note that I am not saying that an action doesn't cre-ate karma that you will have to balance. The karma is created in this world and it has no consequence beyond this world— which as I have said is simply a sandbox designed for your experimentation and designed so that you cannot truly hurt yourself, other beings or the sand. Everything can be erased so you truly do not need to feel any more responsibility for any-thing done in the material world than for building a sand castle on the beach. Once an action and its karma is erased, why feel guilty about it?

As a teacher of Christhood I have no desire for you to feel responsible for actions taken by spirits in your being. My desire is to have you take responsibility for making the choice to create a spirit or allow it to enter your mind. Taking responsibility for an action done by a spirit does nothing to remove that spirit—it actually reinforces the spirit. Taking responsibility for creating the spirit and then choosing to uncreate it will indeed help you grow in self-awareness. Once a spirit is shut out from your being, you are "blameless before God" of all actions taken by that spirit. It is then just a matter of invoking enough spiritual light to balance the energy misqualified through the spirit and that is a finite task.

Again, the ego and the fallen beings want you to take responsibility for what is not your responsibility and keep you from taking responsibility for what is indeed your responsibility. They want you to feel that because you have made certain choices that were bad in an ultimate way, those past choices have taken away your present and future choices. They want you to think that because of something done by a separate spirit, the Conscious You has been irreparably damaged and you can no longer return to pure awareness. This is all a pack of lies.

Spirit cannot be changed by anything in the material universe, and the Conscious You is spirit. Of course, in the here and now, the Conscious You is what it thinks it is. As Shakespeare said, there is nothing good or bad but thinking makes it so. In pure awareness there is nothing good or bad because there is no thinking. There is only oneness and in the singularity of awareness there is no space for thoughts to arise. There is no space for thoughts of blame to arise.

13 | LOVE AND HATE GAMES

What shall one say about love? A wise teacher might say nothing about love. Words belong in the realm of space, and in space there is always room for division. Once there is division, there is room for the mind of anti-christ to define conditions. Once conditions are defined, one has lost love. Perhaps I am not a wise teacher, or perhaps I am wise enough to realize that one can indeed say something about how the ego deals with love.

The ego and the fallen beings are completely blinded by the consciousness of anti-christ and they can think only in terms of opposites. To the mind of anti-christ everything has an opposite. The first step of the fallen beings is to define an opposite to everything—even setting the devil up as the opposite of God (as if the formless could ever have an opposite). If I say "Yes," you can say "No." For any word I might use to describe love, the mind of anti-christ can come up with an opposite. If I say love is unconditional, the mind of anti-christ can say it is conditional, if I say love is infinite one can say it is finite and so on ad infinitum.

The reality that can be experienced by the Conscious You is that the original God qualities, such as the ones represented by the seven rays and beyond them by the secret rays, have no opposites. The mind of anti-christ neither can nor will deal with this fact and it will seek to pervert any God quality. However, a God quality is a form of vibration. In its pure form this vibration is beyond anything found in the material world, which is why it has transformative power.

One might say that it is not possible to pervert a God quality, but it is indeed possible to pervert the *concept* of a God quality. As I have attempted to explain, the Conscious You has the potential to return to its center and experience pure awareness. In pure awareness you can experience each God quality directly and this is the ultimate transformative experience. Until you have such a mystical experience, an experience of gnosis, you will know a God quality only as a concept. When you are dealing with a concept, you are dealing with a mental image of the God quality rather than the indivisible reality. The concept exists in space and thus there is room for it to be divided into two opposing polarities. To the mind of anti-christ everything that is of the Christ mind is a concept and never an experience. It can be endlessly debated and refuted by the mind of anti-christ.

It is easy for most spiritual students to understand that the fallen beings have perverted good by defining something that is clearly evil. What have I said about the dualistic nature of the ego? You must create two aspects. You cannot create one perversion of a God quality, you must create two. What the fallen beings have done is to take the *concept* of the God quality love and then they have created two perversions, namely what human beings call hatred and what human beings call love. Neither of them are the God quality of love.

One of the more subtle ego games is precisely the one which says that as a spiritual person, you need to avoid everything that your spiritual teaching defines as evil and you need to embrace and multiply everything your teaching defines as good. Avoiding dualistic hatred and embracing dualistic love will never get you closer to experiencing the non-dual God quality of love.

Human love is not love

Why isn't human love real love? Because it is in a polarity with hatred and it can be turned into hatred at the blink of an eye. When you have taken human love as far as it can be taken, a disappointment can cause you to instantly swing to the opposite polarity of hatred. Just look at how many people throughout history have engaged in a so-called love relationship only to come to a point of almost instantly switching into hating the person they used to claim that they loved.

How is this possible? It is possible only because the so-called love that the person claimed to feel for the beloved was a conditional love. When the other person no longer lived up to the conditions, or when the first person became aware that the other person never lived up to the conditions, then love was instantly transformed into hatred. The person now felt he or she had been cheated, abused, taken advantage of or deceived. Suddenly, it was now justified to hate the other person and to express this hatred in all kinds of ways that spiritual people know are not spiritual, not kind and not loving.

What is behind human love? It is the ego's desire for control. The human love game is truly a control game where the ego of one person (possibly of both partners) is seeking to control another person by claiming to love that person. It follows that the person who is loved is not loved freely because by accepting a love relationship, he or she has – often without knowing this – submitted to a set of conditions and is now expected to live up to these or feel the repercussions. How is it possible that you can claim to love another person, yet if the person does not live up to the conditions that you have defined (and which the other person may know nothing about), it is suddenly justified that you treat that person in a way no truly loving person would treat another human being? Divine love cannot be turned into hatred so it follows that only human love can flip into its opposite. Again, how do you get off this treadmill? Only by reconnecting to pure awareness so you can experience God love.

The origin of the need for control

Given what I have said about free will, why would you ever think you need to control another person? It is possible only because when you go into separation, you inevitably come to feel incomplete. You adopt what I have called the deficit approach to life. You feel incomplete inside yourself, and you reason that since you do not have what you need inside, you can get it only from some source outside yourself.

This causes most people to approach a love relationship with a deficit of love that makes them feel unwhole and unloved. They have the (often unrecognized) expectation that the other person is going to be able to give them the love that will make them feel loved and whole. They then define a set of conditions (and they are often unconscious and cannot even be communicated to the other person) for what the other person is supposed to do in order to make them feel loved. Right there we have the core of most problems in human relationships.

The fact is that once you go into separation, you will *never* feel whole. No matter how much love another person would give to you, you still would not feel fully loved. It is a simple truth that you will *never* feel whole by receiving something from outside yourself and you will never be whole by receiving something from this world. Human love – in any amount

– will *never* satisfy your need for love. The ego's need for love is a black hole that can never be filled.

You can feel whole only when you experience a God quality. You can feel loved and filled with love only through God love. Which part of you can experience God love? Certainly not the ego and any spirits so that leaves the Conscious You. The Conscious You cannot experience God love through the filter of the ego or any spirits. You can experience God love only when you return to pure awareness.

Here comes the trick. How do you return to pure awareness so you can experience God love? God love is a quality that cannot be owned because it is free and constantly flows. You cannot experience God love as a static quality that you can control, store or possess. You can experience it only as a living stream that flows through you.

How do you experience God love? By being willing to become an open door so that God love can flow through you and be expressed in this world. It is when you are flowing with the stream of God love that you will feel whole and truly loved.

How can God love flow through you? Only when you set no conditions for its flow but are willing to let it express itself freely. Now look at how most people approach a love relationship. They do it with the deficit approach and they think they are entitled to receive something from the person they claim to love. In order to experience God love flowing through you, you need to transcend the deficit approach and engage in a love relationship for the sole purpose of giving to the other person. It is in giving to life here below that you receive more from Above. This is a fundamental law of life.

What is the ideal attitude for entering a love relationship? It is to be willing to give to the other person so that you can receive from God and feel God love flowing through you. This is what most people can do while they are in love, but when a relationship enters the more settled phase, when the honeymoon is over, the ego and the subconscious spirits begin to take over and now the flow of love from inside yourself is suddenly shut off. The reason is that the ego and the spirits have not imposed conditions on your expression of love and this shuts off the flow. That is why I said that you have to become as little children.

No need to control love

Why will the false teachers of this planet endlessly argue against love as being unconditional? Because that which is unconditional cannot be controlled. How do you control anything? By defining conditions and then projecting that people have to conform to those conditions. Those who believe this and seek to conform to your conditions are under your control. The fallen beings are seeking to control people on earth by defining conditions for how everything should be done—even how God would do it or want you to do it.

What is the very core of this attempt? It is the idea that something has gone wrong in this universe and that God or God's qualities cannot correct the problem. Human beings must compensate for this cosmic accident by conforming to the conditions defined by the fallen beings.

What is reality? The reality is that nothing has gone wrong with God's plan. Self-aware beings (fallen and not fallen) have simply exercised their free will. Some have gone into separation where they think they can define their own reality independently of the reality of God. This is allowed by the Law of Free Will, but the only way beings can get out of this illusion is through the School of Hard Knocks. They must take their self-defined "reality" so far into the extremes that they realize it simply does not work and now they want to be free of it. Some believe that it was in rebelling against God's design that they claimed true freedom of will so they must exercise the separate will until they realize that in reality they are imprisoned by it.

What is the only way to be delivered from the illusion of separation? It is to open yourself up to having the God qualities flow through you. A God quality is not stupid. Unconditional love is not some wishy-washy form of love but is highly intelligent or aware. It senses what conditions you have in your mind and then it seeks to take you gradually beyond those conditions. The God qualities can literally help you overcome any problem.

Take note of the subtle distinction. A God quality will never conform to the conditions defined by the fallen mindset. It is not correct to say that the God qualities can solve all problems defined through the mind of anti-christ. Such problems truly have no solution. Once a solution is proposed, that solution will take you towards one dualistic extreme. The more you move towards one extreme, the more you increase the magnetic pull drawing you towards the opposite extreme. The nearer you come to your supposed solution, the more tension you will have in your mind, pulling you away from that solution.

The only solution to human problems is to experience a God quality that offers you an alternative frame of reference. Once you have this, you can see how unreal the dualistic polarities are. The Conscious You can then make a conscious choice to leave behind a set of paired spirits. This takes you one step closer to spiritual freedom, and if you continue the process until all spirits are gone, you are ready to ascend.

You see now that there is no need to control love. Your only choice about God love is whether to let it flow freely or whether to shut it off by accepting conditions from the mind of anti-christ. The mind of anti-christ thinks it can solve any problem, and thus it should be allowed to control the flow of love. If you come to see love as a solution, your ego will immediately begin to define conditions for how you should express it. If you truly want to be free, you need to let go of all conditions so you become the open door that neither man, nor the ego, nor fallen beings can shut. An open door can be open only when it has no conditions for how a God quality should express itself in this world.

The mind of anti-christ – despite its blustering – will never be able to fathom what the mind of Christ can see. A person who is an open door for love may express love in ways that shock other people. Unless you are willing to let love express itself without conditions, you cannot be an open door for love. Unless you become an open door for God love, you cannot be free from the ego's love and hate games. To be free from a treadmill, the Conscious You must make a conscious decision to get off.

I have already made my decision to get off the treadmill of anti-christ. When you make yours, I will be there to help make it a living reality, for I AM the Living Christ.

About the Author

Kim Michaels is an accomplished writer and author. He has conducted spiritual conferences and workshops in 14 countries, has counseled hundreds of spiritual students and has done numerous radio shows on spiritual topics. Kim has been on the spiritual path since 1976. He has studied a wide variety of spiritual teachings and practiced many techniques for raising consciousness. Since 2002 he has served as a messenger for Jesus and other ascended masters. He has brought forth extensive teachings about the mystical path, many of them available for free on his websites: *www.askrealjesus.com, www. ascendedmasteranswers.com, www.ascendedmasterlight.com* and *www.transcendencetoolbox.com.* For personal information, visit Kim at *www.KimMichaels.info.*

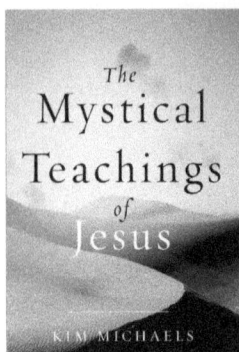

The teachings in this book have helped hundreds of thousands of people gain a deeper appreciation for Jesus's teachings about the mystical path that he taught 2,000 years ago and that he still teaches today—for those who are able to make an inner connection with him.

TODAY MANY PEOPLE CANNOT find a lasting heart connection to the real Jesus and his teachings because, according to most Christian churches, Jesus no longer talks to us. In reality, Jesus is a spiritual being and he is working to help all people who are able to raise their consciousness and attune to his Presence. For the past 2,000 years he has maintained a line of communication through those who have been willing to serve as messengers for his Living Word and who have pursued an understanding of his true message instead of settling for official Christian doctrines.

In this book, the ascended Jesus reveals the mystical teachings that he gave to his most advanced disciples. He explains why his true teachings are as relevant today as they were two millennia ago and how you can develop a personal relationship with him— one of the most remarkable spiritual teachers of all time.

Once you admit that mainstream religious traditions have not answered your questions about life, it is truly liberating to read the deep and meaningful answers in this book. Encouraging, moving and profound, this enlightening book will help you attain inner attunement with Jesus, even mystical union with him.

You will learn how to:
- recognize the silent, inner voice of Christ in your heart
- achieve permanent inner peace and happiness by getting connected with the Christ Consciousness
- heal yourself from emotional wounds
- get guidance from Jesus, who is your greatest teacher and friend
- communicate directly with Jesus

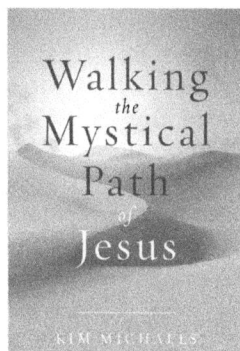

The teachings in this book have helped hundreds of thousands of people gain a deeper appreciation for the mystical path that Jesus taught to his disciples 2000 years ago, the path towards union with God, a state of mind beyond most people's highest dreams.

Walking
the
Mystical
Path
of
Jesus

KIM MICHAELS

TODAY MANY PEOPLE HAVE trouble discovering the small, easy and practical steps towards a state of consciousness that is beyond human conflicts and pitfalls. In this book the ascended master Jesus describes how to start walking the mystical path that will eventually restore our most natural ability: the direct experience of God within ourselves.

This book empowers you to discover your personal path and make steady progress towards peace of mind and an inner, mystical experience of God.

Inspiring and profound, this enlightening book contains questions and answers that are easy to read and that help you walk the mystical path of Jesus.

You will learn how to:

- Use the cosmic mirror to speed up your growth
- Get out of old reactionary patterns
- Become free from difficult situations and guilt
- Control your mind
- Leave behind a painful past
- Open your heart to the flow of love from within
- Heal the wounds in your psychology

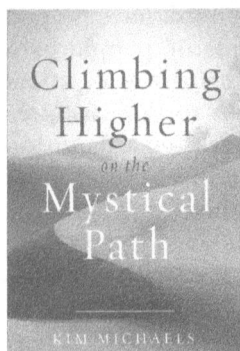

Hundreds of thousands of people have been inspired and uplifted by the profound teachings released in the form of conversations between the ascended master Jesus and Kim Michaels.

IN THIS BOOK JESUS DESCRIBES in a very personal way the more advanced stages of the mystical or spiritual path. Jesus describes through practical examples how our souls get fragmented in different embodiments and how the pieces of the soul get lost when we have experienced deep traumas in this lifetime or during previous lifetimes. The result is that our souls become vulnerable to different soul diseases that reduce our ability to enjoy life fully. Jesus explains how to restore our most natural ability—the ability to communicate with God directly. He skillfully explains how to make completely free choices in a world that seems to be full of toxic emotions and attitudes: fear, pride and guilt. Jesus explains how to overcome the sharpest tool of the dualistic mind—doubt combined with fear and pride.

In an easy to read question and answer form, Jesus guides you to a deeper understanding of how some lifestreams are young and mature, some rebel against God and some seek union with God. He helps you break through the opposition from both outside forces and the inner enemy of the ego.

You will learn how to:
- make use of your closest spiritual teacher – Jesus – on your own mystical path
- turn your past traumatic soul experiences into a forward step
- restore the fragments of your soul and by doing this developing your own direct union with God
- learn from even false teachers and overcome fear, pride and doubt
- avoid being disappointed by spiritual organizations
- create a new identity based on love

Freedom
from
Ego
Illusions

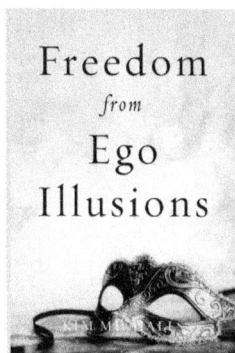

One of the most remarkable spiritual teachers known to humankind is Jesus who taught the mystical path of reunion with God to his disciples 2,000 years ago. Today, Jesus, as an ascended master, teaches that same path to those who are willing to be his modern disciples. Jesus knows that the major obstacle we all face on the mystical journey is the human ego.

THE EGO IS THE MOST SUBTLE CHALLENGE on the spiritual path because it distorts our thoughts, emotions, attitudes, even the way we look at life. In this book Jesus offers his most loving guidance in order to help you rise beyond the level of consciousness affected by the ego. In this new-found freedom, you will be able to grasp the divine vision, both for yourself and for the world you create.

Jesus teaches you how to start seeing through the illusions that the ego uses to keep you trapped in a lower state of consciousness. You will learn:

* How to avoid having your life consumed by an impossible quest
* How to distinguish between the ego itself and its illusions
* How the world view of the ego becomes a self-fulfilling prophecy
* How to rise above the black-and-white thinking of the ego
* How to avoid being trapped in the gray thinking of the ego
* How the ego can use a spiritual teaching to stop your growth
* How to overcome internal divisions that sabotage your growth

You will also find an in-depth discussion about why and how the ego was created. You will learn that you will always have an element of ego as long as you are in embodiment, but that you can come to see through the ego and make creative decisions.